Writing for the Legal Audience

Writing for the Legal Audience

SECOND EDITION

Wayne Schiess

CAROLINA ACADEMIC PRESS

Durham, North Carolina

Library of Congress Cataloging-in-Publication Data

Schiess, Wayne, 1963- author.
  Writing for the legal audience / Wayne Schiess. -- Second edition.
    p. cm.
  Includes bibliographical references and index.
  ISBN 978-1-61163-391-7 (alk. paper)
  1. Legal composition. I. Title.

KF250.S35 2014
808.06'634--dc23   2013032765

Carolina Academic Press
700 Kent Street
Durham, North Carolina 27701
Telephone (919) 489-7486
Fax (919) 493-5668
Email: cap@cap-press.com
www.cap-press.com

Printed in the United States of America

For Kimberli

Contents

Writing for the Legal Audience

Chapter 1

Audience

Who is my audience?

You should answer that question first on any legal-writing project. I hope this book will prompt you to think about audience on every project because the measure of good legal writing is whether the audience gets the message. It doesn't matter if your document looks or sounds "legal." What matters is that it conveys the legal meaning to the intended audience. To me, the only good legal writing is audience-focused writing. I hope you agree.

I also hope you detect the major themes in this book—the broad principles that drive audience-focused writing. Mainly there are three:

- *Write naturally.* Good legal writing is readable and natural and direct. It's not overly formal, esoteric, or pompous.
- *Make information accessible.* In legal writing, the most important information should be up front. Other information should be well organized and clearly signposted.
- *Consult the authorities.* When you have questions about writing, don't guess. Look things up. That's what professional writers do.

If you target your audience and remember these principles, your legal writing will be a cut above the ordinary.

Chapter 2

Writing to the Prospective Employer

- *Aim for perfect prose.*
- *Be concrete.*
- *Be accurate.*

Whether you're just coming out of law school or are 30 years into practice, when the opportunity or need arises to apply for a job, you want to make a good first impression. Any employer will read your written materials carefully, but legal employers are especially justified in closely scrutinizing your cover letter and résumé. After all, according to the legal-writing expert Joseph Kimble, effective written communication is one of the most important of all legal skills.[1] So sweat over your cover letter and résumé as if they were critical documents prepared for a valuable client. They are.

1. Aim for perfect prose.

Even though your résumé is probably the most important part of your written application, your cover letter is what the prospective employer will see first. Don't assume the employer won't read it. Because it is your first chance to make an impression, the prose in your cover letter ought to be smooth, readable, and error-free. To present the most polished prose you can, follow these suggestions for cover letters:

- Use impeccably correct grammar, punctuation, and spelling.
- Use direct words instead of qualifiers and intensifiers.
- Choose the right words and avoid trendy ones.

---

1. Joseph Kimble, *On Legal-Writing Programs*, 2 Perspectives: Teaching Leg. Res. & Writing 43 (1994).

Let's put these suggestions into practice. Read the following actual cover letter, in which I've changed the name of the prospective employer. The applicant seeks an entry-level associate position.

Dear Mr. Scheiss:

The opportunity to pursue an associate position with Scheiss & Associates is extremely attractive to me. The firm's reputation as an innovative and forward-thinking organization is quite admirable. I am very interested in learning more about the firm and in bringing my personal strengths to your firm.

My strong liberal arts background and extensive leadership experience has served to enhance my analytical, communication and writing abilities. Through extracurricular activities and volunteer work, I have gained valuable insight into the dynamics of working with others. Multiple internships with a major law firm gave me practical experience in combining verbal and written skills with the specific needs of the firm. A well-rounded learning experience at King's College in London also honed my analytical and communication abilities.

I am eager to attain an opportunity to extend the qualities I have to offer to Scheiss & Associates. Your consideration of my candidacy as an associate is much appreciated. I look forward to the opportunity to discuss further how my qualities are a fit with Scheiss & Associates.

Sincerely,

Now let's assess the strength of this letter on the three suggestions for polished prose.

Grammar, punctuation, and spelling

Readers with whom you have an established relationship might forgive a minor spelling mistake or a slight grammatical flaw. But in a letter asking for a job from someone you don't know, you can't afford to let anything—even a missing comma—distract the employer from the good impression you're trying to make.

You probably noticed some grammar, punctuation, and spelling mistakes in this letter. I noted these:

Text	Problem	Comment
Scheiss	Spelling	Ouch! You'd better not misspell the name of the person you're addressing. Triple-check it.
liberal arts background and extensive leadership experience **has** served	Verb agreement; *has* should be *have*.	Because the sentence has a compound subject (two nouns—*background* and *experience*), the verb must be plural.
analytical, communication and writing abilities	Serial comma; the phrase should be *analytical, communication, and writing abilities* with a comma before the *and.*	Outside legal writing, (in literature and journalism, for example), the serial comma (the comma before the conjunction in a series of three or more) is optional. But legal writing is a form of technical writing, so get in the habit of using the serial comma; nearly every legal-writing and technical-writing book recommends it.*

See, e.g., Anne Enquist & Laurel Currie Oates, *Just Writing: Grammar, Punctuation, & Style for the Legal Writer* 224–225 (3d ed. Aspen L. & Bus. 2009); Patricia T. O'Conner, *Woe is I: The Grammarphobe's Guide to Better English in Plain English* 137 (Riverhead Books 1996); Gary Blake & Robert Bly, *The Elements of Technical Writing* 49–50 (Macmillan 1993); Martha Faulk & Irving Mehler, *The Elements of Legal Writing* 69 (Macmillan 1994).

Any one of these problems could distract the reader from your qualifications. So edit carefully and proofread thoroughly. It may help to have another person read the cover letter to check for errors. A fresh set of eyes will often catch the small mistakes you missed.

Strong, direct words instead of intensifiers

Perhaps it's counterintuitive, but intensifiers—like *extremely*—tend to weaken prose, not intensify it. This letter has four intensifiers, *extremely*, *quite*, *very*, and *much*. Not only do they fail to strengthen the writing, they weary the reader because there are so many of them. If everything in the letter is *extremely* something or *very* something, the intensifying effect is lost.

In all four cases in this letter, the sentence is fine without the intensifier. In fact, all four sentences are more than fine; they're better if we omit the intensifier. So leave out the intensifier or choose a stronger word that doesn't need intensifying.

The right word

It's wise to get a good dictionary and use it. But dictionaries can tell you only what a word *means*. If you want to know how a word ought to be *used*, you'll need a *usage* dictionary. Usage dictionaries will also teach you about grammar and style; they'll tell you what words and phrases are misused, inflated, or outdated; and they'll explain common errors and misspellings. Here are three I recommend:

- Bryan A. Garner, *Garner's Modern American Usage* (3d ed., Oxford U. Press 2009)
- Mark Davidson, *Right, Wrong, and Risky: A Dictionary of Today's American English Usage* (Norton 2005)
- H. W. Fowler, *A Dictionary of Modern English Usage* (2d ed., Ernest Gowers, ed., Oxford U. Press 1965)

Every lawyer ought to have a usage dictionary.

The usage concerns in the original letter are minor, but both could distract the reader:

Word	Problem	Comment
dynamics	This is a trendy or "vogue" word, according to Garner.*	If it is a vogue word, many other writers are using it. Make your letter stand out by not choosing the vogue word.
attain	Probably not the meaning the writer wants here.	Attain means "to gain or accomplish."** Here, the writer is asking for something, not accomplishing something. The usage is awkward.

    * Bryan A. Garner, *Garner's Modern American Usage* 286 (3d ed., Oxford U. Press 2009)
    ** *The Oxford Dictionary & Thesaurus* 84 (Am. ed., Oxford U. Press 1996).

A revision containing all the changes recommended in this first section appears in the next section.

2. Be concrete.

Providing specific details brings emphasis to your points, and vague generalities get lost in the reader's mind. They simply do not stand out. For example, if you want to tell the reader about the extra things you've done that set you apart, you might write:

> Through **extracurricular activities** and **volunteer work**, I have gained valuable insight ...

But readers will quickly forget that vague and general statement. Or worse, it will annoy: What activities? What volunteer work? The reader does not get a picture to remember or an image to keep in mind. If you really want to emphasize the extra things you've done, you'd be more successful if you wrote this:

> Through **working on The Journal of Appellate Practice** and **volunteering at the law school writing clinic**, I have gained valuable insight ...

This vivid sentence provides concrete details that a reader can "see." Most lawyers will know exactly what it means to work on a journal. And it's easy to picture you advising students who have come to the clinic with writing questions.

On the other hand, providing too much detail can bore the reader and pointlessly lengthen the text. To explain the extra things you've done, you probably wouldn't write this:

> As a staffer on the Journal of Appellate Practice, I participated in 11 cite-checks in the second semester of my second year. I supervised eight more during the first semester of my third year. One of the cite-checks was novel because we needed to find a rare international treaty one of the authors had cited....

That's tedious. So when writing to a prospective employer, be concrete about your accomplishments, be specific about your activities, and explain what you can do — without excessive detail.

Here's our cover letter again. I've corrected the errors discussed in section 1, and highlighted the vague, nonspecific phrases.

> Dear Mr. Schiess:
>
> The opportunity to pursue an associate position with Schiess & Associates is attractive to me. The firm's reputation as **an innovative and forward-thinking organization** is admirable. I am interested in learning more about the firm and in bringing **my personal strengths** to your firm.
>
> My strong **liberal arts background** and **extensive leadership experience** have served to enhance my analytical, communication, and writing abilities. Through **extracurricular activities** and **volunteer work**, I have gained valuable insight into effectively working with others. Multiple internships with **a major law firm** gave me practical experience in combining

verbal and written skills with **the specific needs of the firm.**
A **well-rounded learning experience at King's College** in London also honed my analytical and communication abilities.

I am eager for an opportunity to extend the qualities I have to offer to Schiess & Associates. Your consideration of my candidacy as an associate is appreciated. I look forward to the opportunity to discuss further how my qualities are a fit with Schiess & Associates.

Sincerely,

Now that I've highlighted the general, non-detailed statements, it really ought to strike you how weak those statements are. The thinking reader is left with many questions. Here are the most glaring general statements and the questions a reader might have:

Statement	Reader's question
An innovative and forward-thinking organization	What is it about the firm that makes it innovative and forward-thinking?
my personal strengths	Which are?
liberal arts background	A vague statement; what field, specifically?
extensive leadership experience	What *was* that experience?
volunteer work	Of what kind?
major law firm	Which one? Now I'm wondering if there's a reason you're not naming it.
needs of the firm	What needs?
extracurricular activities	What were those activities? Were any of them relevant to law practice?

This letter prompts many questions, and the reader might justifiably be annoyed when first reading it. Nothing specific is ever mentioned.

Granted, the résumé will answer some of these questions, but this writer risks having the employer move on to someone else with a more memorable cover letter. Or if there are three dozen applicants, the writer risks having this letter fade into the mass of typical, general covers.

And now that I've highlighted the general statements, we see that the writer has probably brought up too many subjects for a short cover letter. The writer would be well advised to pick two or three strengths, mention them—with specific details—and stop.

For the revision, I won't worry about length; instead, I'll offer a revision that includes details for all the general statements. For purposes of the revision, assume that Schiess & Associates is an appellate-practice boutique. Here is the revised letter:

> Dear Mr. Schiess:
>
> The opportunity to pursue an associate position with Schiess & Associates is attractive to me. The firm's reputation for **producing high-caliber appellate briefs** is admirable. I am interested in learning more about the firm and in bringing **my writing strengths** to your firm.
>
> My **college degree in English** and **my work as vice president of the law school student body** have served to enhance my analytical, communication, and writing abilities. Through **working on The Journal of Appellate Practice** and **volunteering at the law school writing clinic,** I have gained valuable insight into effectively working with others. Multiple internships with **Williams & Hanna, LLP** gave me practical experience in using verbal and written skills in **a general practice.** My semester at King's College in London, **where I wrote three seminar papers,** also honed my analytical and communication abilities.

* * *

This new letter tells us a lot about the qualifications that make the applicant a strong candidate. It's much more memorable; it's distinct from the run-of-the-mill cover letters the employer probably sees. And it invites better questions: instead of "what kind of volunteer work did you do?" the employer can ask "what writing weaknesses did you see in the students at the clinic?"

In short, it gives the reader's mind something to hold on to.

3. Be accurate and honest.

When you write to a prospective employer, you're representing yourself. Of course, when you're representing a client you must be honest in your dealings with others. The ABA Model Rules of Professional Conduct require it: "[A] lawyer shall not knowingly ... make a false statement of material fact ... to a third person."[2]

But what about when you're representing yourself—in the letter to a prospective employer or in your résumé? Is honesty necessary? Perhaps it could go without saying, but accuracy and honesty are required there, too. Deception in the cover letter or résumé can cost you the job and can result in bar discipline.

To drive the point home, let me share with you some real-life examples of the dishonest things lawyers have written. All these lawyers received bar discipline or were held civilly liable for fraud:

- In an application for a law-school teaching position, the lawyer wrote that he was first in his class when he was 25th, that he was Editor-in-Chief of the law review when he was merely on the editorial board, and that he was a member of the Order of the Coif when he was not.[3]
- The lawyer's résumé, sent to win a potential client, said that he had opened his practice in 1991 when it was actually 1994, that he had represented healthcare organizations when he had not, and that he was licensed in New Jersey and Massachusetts when he was not.[4]
- The lawyer's résumé said he had graduated from Yale when he was actually two credits short of graduation.[5]

---

2. Model Rules of Professional Conduct 4.1(a) (ABA 1996).
3. *In re Hadzi-Antich*, 497 A.2d 1062, 1064 (D.C. Ct. App. 1985).
4. *Baker v. Dorfman*, 239 F.3d 415, 425 (2d Cir. 2000).
5. *In re Norwood*, 438 N.Y.S.2d 788, 788 (N.Y. App. Div. 1981).

These lawyers paid a high price for their deception and exaggeration. Learn from their mistakes; be scrupulously honest in what you write when applying for a job.

If you proofread carefully, if you strive to be concrete and specific about who you are and what you can do, and if you always tell the truth, your job application will stand out. It will interest the prospective employer. It will impress.

Chapter 3

Writing to the Supervisor

- *Answer questions directly.*
- *Be succinct.*
- *Be thorough.*

This chapter is directed to those who must write for a boss or supervising attorney. Its aim is to improve your ability to report on what your supervisor asked you and to make that report an effective decision-making tool. The most common way lawyers report to their supervisors is in the traditional legal memorandum.

But describing how to write a complete legal memo is beyond the scope of this book. To do so would mean long explanations of how to do legal research and how to organize and present a legal analysis. Instead, I'll focus on what I believe is the most important part of the legal memo: the conclusion. The conclusion is most important because it is usually the first thing—and sometimes the only thing—your supervisor will read. And I believe that if your conclusion is well written, the rest of the memo will be better, too.

I offer three suggestions to make your conclusions efficient, accessible, and easy to read. Those things are important because of the most universal trait of the supervisor audience: supervisors are always in a hurry. They are busy. They want good information, but they want it fast.

1. Answer questions directly.

The most important part of any memo is the conclusion—where you answer the question you were asked. It's the reason the supervisor gave you the assignment in the first place. Your supervisor isn't testing your ability to state the question or recite the facts. And though your supervisor *is* going to assess your legal analysis, that analysis is worthless if you can't answer the question directly—if you can't state the conclusion well.

Answering questions directly requires you to do two things:

- Avoid delay; give the answer first, the qualifiers and reasons afterward.
- Avoid unnecessary hedging; state the answer with as much certainty as you can.

To highlight these two suggestions, let's consider a real-world example. Imagine that a lawyer was given an assignment to write a memo answering this question:

Question Presented

In Illinois, in-house counsel who are fired may not sue their employers—who are also their clients—for retaliatory discharge. Donnette Green worked at a small law firm that had one client; the client treated the lawyers like in-house counsel. She reported on a partner she suspected was overbilling the client. She was fired. Can Green's suit for retaliatory discharge survive summary judgment?

Now consider this answer, which I've labeled *Conclusion*, which we'll imagine appears directly below the Question Presented on the first page of the memo.

Conclusion

The Illinois cases of *Balla v. Gambro, Inc.*, 584 N.E.2d 104 (Ill. 1991) and *Herbster v. North American Co. for Life & Health Insurance*, 501 N.E.2d 343 (Ill. App. Ct. 1987), directly impact this issue, though these cases are ten and fourteen years old respectively. However, research has revealed that recent Illinois precedent has not displaced their holdings. Moreover, although both the precedent cases held that despite the fact that regular employees are entitled to sue for retaliatory discharge on the theory that it will provide an incentive for employees to "blow the whistle" on activities that could be harmful to the public or that are illegal, attorneys are not entitled to the same right of action. Nevertheless, under the circumstances described, a possible action by Ms. Green could well be allowed to go forward. This is because although in-house counsel have been treated by the *Balla* and *Herbster* courts as having an independent, ethical obligation to disclose harmful activity, and hence no need for the incentive provided by a retaliatory-discharge cause of action, Ms. Green did not represent her employer as a lawyer, as in-house counsel do. Therefore, she is not under the same ethical obligation to disclose harmful activities, and hence deserves the incentives provided by the retaliatory-discharge suit.

First of all, at 210 words it's not a quick read, is it? But we'll leave that for section two of this chapter. Now to our suggestions for answering directly.

Avoid delay.

The very first words of the conclusion ought to tell the supervisor the answer to the question. That makes sense, right? Yet much of what lawyers write—whether in memos, letters, or court documents—fails to give the answer first. That's a weakness you should especially avoid when writing for a supervisor. Not much will frustrate a supervisor more than trying to wade through a conclusion like our example conclusion here.

If you look at this example closely, you'll realize that the answer ("a possible action by Ms. Green could well be allowed to go forward") is buried in the middle of the paragraph. That's the worst possible place for it. The legal reader will expect it to be up front; if it's not, the next place the reader will look is at the end. If it's not there, either, you've doubly frustrated your supervisor by "hiding" the answer and by forcing the supervisor to reread in search of the answer. To avoid causing these headaches, always state a direct answer in the first sentence—preferably in the first word. And keep it short.

How?

First, phrase your question presented so that it lends itself to a *yes* or *no* answer. I realize that may not be possible for all assignments. For example, your supervisor might ask an opened-ended question, like "What does the Idaho Products Liability Act provide?" Obviously, you can't answer that *yes* or *no*. But whenever you can, pose a yes-or-no question to set yourself up for a clear conclusion.

Second, answer with a short, direct word or phrase whenever you can. Not all legal questions can appropriately be answered *yes* or *no*, but nearly all can be answered somewhere along the following simple continuum, suggested by John Dernbach and his coauthors in their popular legal-writing text.[1]

Yes——Probably yes——Probably not——No

Our conclusion would be much better if we started with a direct answer from this continuum and moved the sentence that contains the prediction from the middle to the beginning. We'll also drop the word *nevertheless* because we don't need a transition word. Here's our revised first sentence:

Probably yes. Under the circumstances described, a possible action by Ms. Green could well be allowed to go forward.

This is much better. The busy supervisor has a clear answer right up front. And now that we have highlighted the answer in boldface type, let's leave it that way. The legal-writing expert Terri LeClercq suggests it as a way to draw the reader's attention quickly.[2]

Avoid unnecessary hedging.

Your supervisor will appreciate it if you state the answer to the question with as much legal certainty as is warranted. How much is warranted? That depends on what you find in your research. With experience, you'll become better at predicting what a judge, an appellate panel, or a prosecutor might do.

But no matter how experienced you are, you can still do better simply by the way you phrase the answer. Usually, an answer that be-

---

1. John C. Dernbach, Richard V. Singleton, Cathleen S. Wharton, & Joan M. Ruhtenberg, *A Practical Guide to Legal Writing & Legal Method* 189 (2d ed., Fred B. Rothman 1994).

2. *See* Terri LeClercq, *Guide to Legal Writing Style* 101 (2d ed., Aspen L. & Bus. 2000).

gins with *yes* or *no* is the best approach, as I've suggested. In general, prefer those direct answers whenever appropriate.

Often though, lawyers want to hedge the answer. After all, the answer is usually a prediction of future events, and lawyers know that almost nothing is certain, least of all the law. Besides, your supervisor wouldn't have given you the assignment if there were a simple, clear answer; so you know it's probably a close call. Rather than take a strong, yes-or-no position and be wrong, you might try to hedge; it just feels safer to qualify the answer. But the hedged answer is weaker and less effective as a decision-making tool for the supervisor. So qualify your answer only when you must.

Another tip: don't let knee-jerk, stereotypical qualifiers creep into your writing. Many experts recommend avoiding over-used qualifiers, including Bryan Garner and Steven Stark. Common qualifying words and phrases they suggest guarding against are

- *it would appear that, it might be said that, it is respectfully suggested that*[3]
- *seems, apparently, maybe*[4]

Yet sometimes you must qualify the answer—an absolute *yes* or *no* won't do. In his book, *Writing to Win*, Steven Stark says that when you qualify your answer, you must always explain clearly why.[5] Don't leave a qualification unexplained.

Our example conclusion fails on both accounts: it is unnecessarily qualified, and we must infer the reason for the qualification from the sentences *before* the answer. For example, consider this sentence from our conclusion:

---

3. Bryan A. Garner, *The Elements of Legal Style* 36 (2d ed., Oxford U. Press 2002).

4. Steven D. Stark, *Writing to Win: The Legal Writer* 44 (2d ed., Three Rivers Press 2012).

5. Stark, *Writing to Win* at 45.

Under the circumstances described, a possible action by Ms. Green could well be allowed to go forward.

Here's an analysis of this sentence:

Phrase	Comment	Suggestion
under the circumstances described	It properly limits the prediction to the facts of this scenario, but is that necessary? What other scenario could the supervisor have in mind?	Omit
a possible action by Ms. Green	Is it necessary to say that the action is *possible*? What the writer probably means is that we don't know if Ms. Green will sue. So say *if*.	If Ms. Green sues ...
could well be allowed to go forward	*Could* is imprecise. Lots of things *could* happen, but will they? And *could well* is just fluff. *Allowed to go forward* is also vague. We'll fix that in part three of this chapter.	Probably

So now the sentence would read:

If Ms. Green sues, the suit will probably be allowed to go forward.

The very next sentence ought to explain why the answer is "probably." Here, the reason the answer is "probably" is that two strong precedents have denied lawyers a right to sue for retaliatory discharge. That reason should be explained more concretely than it is and should come after the answer — or we should move the answer to the beginning. We'll do those things in part 2.

2. Be succinct.

The original conclusion had 210 words. By my standards, that's not short enough. How long should a conclusion be? Let's compare the conclusion to its counterpart, the question presented (or issue statement). Bryan Garner's guidelines for writing a question presented suggest that it ought to be 75 words or fewer.[6] Should the conclusion be much longer?

No, but you may need more room because you have to give the reasons. So let's give ourselves 100 words for a conclusion; that's a good goal, not a rigid rule. And think what that means: if the question and conclusion together are 175 words or fewer, the reader gets the question and its answer within 45 seconds—60 seconds at the most. That's worth trying for.

Original	Comment
The Illinois cases of *Balla v. Gambro, Inc.*, 584 N.E.2d 104 (Ill. 1991) and *Herbster v. North American Co. for Life & Health Insurance*, 501 N.E.2d 343 (Ill. App. Ct. 1987)	Generally, avoid citing cases in the conclusion. Doing so adds clutter and length. The supervisor knows the full citations will be in the analysis. Just give the answer here. If the cases are particularly important, mention them by shorthand reference.
directly impact this issue, though these cases are ten and fourteen years old respectively.	First, just mentioning them tells the supervisor they "directly impact" the issue. But if you must say something, say they are important. Second, give the age of a case later, in the analysis (where the date in the parenthetical is enough), unless its age is crucial to the conclusion. If so, refer to the cases like this: "The 1991 *Balla* opinion ..."
However, research has revealed that recent Illinois precedent has not displaced their holdings.	We can save this for the analysis, or it could be shortened to "the cases are still good law."

---

6. Bryan A. Garner, *Legal Writing in Plain English* 58 (U. Chicago Press 2001).

Original	Comment
Moreover, although both the precedent cases held that despite the fact that regular employees are entitled to sue for retaliatory discharge on the theory that it will provide an incentive for employees to "blow the whistle" on activities that could be harmful to the public or that are illegal, attorneys are not entitled to the same right of action.	A 59-word sentence. Too long. But the reasoning provided here is important. We should tell the busy supervisor about the policy behind retaliatory discharge and why that policy doesn't apply to lawyers. Specific suggestions: omit *moreover* or choose a shorter transition; replace *despite the fact that* with *even though*; replace *are entitled to* with *may*; replace *on the theory that* with *because*; replace *activities that could be harmful to the public or that are illegal* with *harmful or illegal activities*; rephrase *attorneys are not entitled to the same right of action* into *attorneys may not*; break the sentence into two.
This is because although in-house counsel have been treated by the *Balla* and *Herbster* courts as having an independent, ethical obligation to disclose harmful activity, and hence no need for the incentive provided by a retaliatory discharge cause of action, Ms. Green did not represent her employer as a lawyer, as in-house counsel do.	A 54-word sentence. Omit the weak opener *this is because*. Instead of *treated by the* Balla *and* Herbster *courts*, just state what the courts have held.
Therefore, she is not under the same ethical obligation to disclose harmful activities, and hence deserves the incentive provided by the retaliatory-discharge suit.	This sentence is acceptable, but by now the conclusion has used three different terms for a lawsuit: *cause of action*, *right of action*, and *suit*. Pick one.

Our original conclusion uses big words, long sentences, and lawyerly sounding phrases. Plus, it contains some detail we can save for the analysis. Now that we've improved the first sentence, let's take the rest of the text, line by line, and tighten it.

With these suggestions in mind, here's a revised conclusion:

> **Probably yes. If Ms. Green sues, the suit will probably be allowed to go forward.** Two Illinois cases, *Balla* in 1991 and *Herbster* in 1987, are important here and are still good law.

They held that even though regular employees may sue for retaliatory discharge because it provides an incentive to "blow the whistle" on harmful or illegal activities, attorney employees such as in-house counsel may not sue. In-house counsel have an independent, ethical obligation to disclose harmful activity; there is no need for the incentive of a retaliatory-discharge suit. But Ms. Green did not represent her employer as a lawyer, as in-house counsel do. Therefore, she is not under the same ethical obligation to disclose harmful activity and deserves the incentives provided by the retaliatory-discharge suit.

That conclusion is 128 words. Not bad. But let's take out the reference to *Balla* and *Herbster*, reorder it so that the reasons follow the answer, and see how much we can improve it:

> **Probably yes. If Ms. Green sues, the suit will probably be allowed to go forward.** Ms. Green did not represent her employer as a lawyer, as in-house counsel do. In-house counsel have an independent, ethical obligation to disclose harmful activities. They do not need the incentive of a retaliatory discharge suit, which encourages regular employees to "blow the whistle." Because Ms. Green was not representing her employer as a lawyer and was not ethically obligated to disclose the harmful activity, she deserves the incentive of the retaliatory discharge suit.

That conclusion is 89 words, gives the answer first and the reasons next, and is much clearer and more succinct than the original.

3. Be thorough.

One day, when I was working as an associate at a large law firm, a senior associate I knew approached me and asked me to work on a memo. He handed me a memo that someone else had written — another associate at the firm — but I did not know who. He implied that the memo was not finished and that the analysis needed to be fleshed out and the prose polished. I got started on it right away and didn't think much about it at first.

The next day, as I worked on the memo—which I thought was not very thorough—it dawned on me that I was rewriting a finished memo produced by another lawyer. The supervisor had been unhappy with the caliber of the memo, so he was having it rewritten. I got a sick feeling in my stomach. I felt bad for my unknown colleague, but I also wondered if any of my memos had been assigned to another lawyer to rewrite.

I learned from that experience, and so I offer this advice: be thorough. Research carefully, write thoughtfully, and proofread several times. Be sure any memo you write won't need to be rewritten.

Three suggestions:

Never turn in a "draft."

No matter what the supervisor says, do not turn in something that is half done, half proofread, or half right. Realize that when supervisors tell you to turn in a "draft," they don't mean a "rough draft." As Robert White put it in his humorous book, *The Official Lawyer's Handbook*:

> [When a supervisor tells you to] "Just get me a *quick* draft," "Just *whip off* a draft," or "Just dictate a *rough* draft" ... [t]he emphasized words should trigger flashing red lights in your mind.[7]

Ask for more time if you must, or stay up all night, but always show your supervisor your best work.

Have a trusted colleague read your memo.

Can a junior attorney ask another attorney to read and comment on a memo draft? Yes. As with all writing, a second set of eyes will often catch the mistakes, glitches, and blunders you missed. If the person you ask to read your memo is well acquainted with the su-

---

7. D. Robert White, *The Official Lawyer's Handbook* 109–110 (Pocket Books 1983).

pervisor, you may also get some insight into what the supervisor looks for, likes, and dislikes.

Pay attention to what you were asked.

Did you notice that our question presented, which appeared in section one of this chapter, was set in a particular procedural posture? Specifically, it asked

> Could Green's suit for retaliatory discharge *survive summary judgment*?

Asking whether a suit can survive summary judgment is different from asking whether it can win outright or whether it can "go forward" as the original conclusion put it. What does "go forward" mean, anyway? Does it mean the plaintiff has standing? Or the plaintiff can survive a motion to dismiss? It's not clear.

The point is that the conclusion didn't address the specific procedural posture of summary judgment at all. Glossing over the procedural posture of what you were asked may slide sometimes, but it isn't "thorough." So be thorough. A careful writer pays attention to the question the supervisor asked.

What might our conclusion look like if we incorporated the summary judgment aspect?

> **Probably yes. Ms. Green's suit can probably survive summary judgment.** Ms. Green did not represent her employer as a lawyer, as in-house counsel do. In-house counsel have an independent, ethical obligation to disclose harmful activities. They do not need the incentive of a retaliatory discharge suit, which encourages regular employees to "blow the whistle." Because Ms. Green was not representing her employer as a lawyer and was not ethically obligated to disclose the harmful activity, she deserves the incentive of the retaliatory discharge suit. Because her situation is not addressed in the case law, her suit would probably get to the jury. (104 words.)

This conclusion should make any supervisor happy.

Remember: When you write the conclusion section of a legal memo, your relationship with your supervisor is at stake, and your credibility is on the line. So be direct, be succinct, and be thorough. Your supervisor will thank you.

Chapter 4

Writing to the E-mail Recipient

- *Be considerate and professional.*
- *Think, pause, think again. Send.*
- *Frontload your content.*

E-mail is pervasive and unavoidable. If those descriptions seem negative, they are—a little. An in-house technology lawyer told me he considers e-mail to be the worst thing that's ever happened to legal writing.

But for many lawyers, like me, it's the preferred way to communicate: messages sent when I want, messages retrieved when I want, and no awkward telephone moments. Yet e-mail has drawbacks. Many lawyers wonder how to manage the huge number of e-mail messages they receive. Some lawyers wonder about the appropriate level of formality—are e-mails like phone messages, like texting, or like formal correspondence? And confidentiality and privacy also concern many lawyers; hence the often stuffily worded warnings that appear at the bottom of every message.

Here are three recommendations for writing good legal e-mails.

1. Be considerate and professional.

Part of the reason we prefer e-mail is that it's easy. But because it's easy, we perhaps use it less carefully than we should on occasion. So here are four professional pointers to keep in mind when using e-mail. Note: the advice here is for professional, work-related e-mail in a law office, not for personal e-mail.

First, keep it short. Most people don't like to receive, or read, long e-mail messages. So be brief. How brief? It's hard to give a firm rule on e-mail length. I like the "no scrolling" rule, also called the "one-screen" rule: in an article for law students, Kelly Watkins suggests writing your e-mail messages so readers won't have to scroll down to read the whole message.[1] That's a tough guideline to follow because you can't predict the recipient's screen size. But at least it reminds you to keep it short.

Second, be professional. In all your work e-mail, maintain the right level of professionalism. It's possible to be too informal, particularly with e-mail, as Gary Blake and Robert W. Bly point out in *The Elements of Technical Writing:*

> Since E-mail is so informal, there is a tendency to write in short, staccato sentences and phrases ... and generally to ignore the rules of punctuation and spacing. Appearance still counts. Treat your e-mail the same as any other professional communication.[2]

Third, consider your options. If the immediacy of e-mail pushes you to respond quickly, resist. As you'll learn in part 3 of this chapter, there are benefits to taking your time. So especially if you're angry or defensive, Blake and Bly recommend giving yourself some time before you respond.[3] In fact, even when you're not angry, you'd do well to take your time anytime you send an e-mail in your capacity as a lawyer.

Fourth, be audience-focused. Write the kind of e-mail you like to receive, and no matter who your audience is, assume that audience will judge you by your e-mail. Every e-mail message you send on the job says something about you and your professionalism.

---

1. Kelly J. Watkins, *Leave Your Smileys at School,* 29 Student Law. 24, 26 (May 2001).

2. Gary Blake & Robert W. Bly, *The Elements of Technical Writing* 141 (Macmillan 1993).

3. *Id.*

2. Think, pause, think again. Send.

Thinking and pausing may not seem to have much to do with composing an e-mail message, but I've included this "thinking" advice because e-mail is so easy to use—and overuse. I've intentionally broken this stage into three steps. If you follow these three steps, your e-mails will be better written and better received.

Think about whether you should use e-mail at all.

Perhaps much of the e-mail volume that clogs our computers could be eliminated if we took the time to consider other options before we sent. If we paused, we would reduce e-mail errors, too, according to Lynne Agress, author of *Working with Words in Business and Legal Writing*:

> The advent of e-mail ... has encouraged just about everyone to try his or her hand at writing off-the-cuff, with little or no preparation or forethought. As a result, lawyers, architects, accountants—all business people, in fact—have been given an equal opportunity to embarrass themselves.[4]

Often a real letter is better than an e-mail because no matter how formally worded the e-mail message is, it will still be less formal than a hard-copy letter. If the formality and seriousness of a real letter is called for, then use it.

Maybe a phone call would be better than an e-mail message. Do you find yourself using e-mail to avoid phone-calling? I do. Often, that's fine. It's one of the reasons many lawyers like e-mail. But at least stop and think about whether a phone call might be more effective. After all, in a phone call you'll have the opportunity for a real-time exchange of information and for conversational context, things that are lacking in a thread of e-mail replies. As Mary A. DeVries wrote in *The Elements of Correspondence*:

---

4. Lynne Agress, *Working with Words in Business and Legal Writing* 105 (Perseus Publishing 2002).

E-mail, because of its speed, is often used, or misused, for messages that should be conveyed face to face, through a personal telephone call, or in a personal handwritten message. It would be inappropriate, for example, to send a message of sympathy, a congratulatory message, or a thank you note by e-mail. Certain messages require a warmer, more human touch than the cold, technical approach that electronic messaging portrays to many people.[5]

So before shooting off an e-mail, consider all three of these options—a letter, a phone call, and a personal visit—especially in the formal context of law practice. You'll reduce e-mail volume generally, and you'll often save yourself regret, embarrassment, and headaches.

Pause long enough to review the message and correct writing errors.

Not enough of us do this. If you use e-mail heavily, these words, from *Get to the Point!* by writing consultant Elizabeth Danziger, will ring true:

> Spelling errors, grammar gaffes, and fuzzy logic are careening through cyberspace at an awful rate. Even people who would ordinarily revise an important letter many times think nothing of pressing "send" to "distribution" without giving their message a second glance. Then their typos and garbled ideas pop straight into the computer terminals of their increasingly impatient colleagues all over the world.[6]

So read your message before you send it. Revise it. Take just a moment to polish it, and you'll save yourself the discomfort of seeing it

---

5. Mary A. DeVries, *The Elements of Correspondence: How to Express Yourself Clearly, Persuasively, and Eloquently in Your Personal and Business Writing* 28 (Macmillan 1994).

6. Elizabeth Danziger, *Get to the Point! Painless Advice for Writing Memos, Letters, and E-mails Your Colleagues and Clients will Understand* 221 (Three Rivers Press 2001).

again—when it comes back in a reply—and wincing at your own errors.

If typos and garbled ideas were the only problems, we might not get too worked up. A bigger problem—according to many practicing lawyers—is the content of the e-mail messages. Too often, lawyers see these problems:

- Sending sensitive or confidential information that should not be sent at all.
- Sending sensitive or confidential information to a list instead of to an individual.
- Sending sensitive or confidential information to the wrong person.
- Sending mistaken or unsubstantiated information.

Once again, pausing for a moment can spare you the headache and embarrassment of making a mistake that hurts your client or displeases your boss.

Sometimes the ramifications can be dramatic: consider this incident, reported in the *New York Times* in April 2002. Someone at a major New York City law firm—a lawyer, probably—destroyed the confidentiality of the bidding process for a bankrupt client by using e-mail carelessly. This person was sending a routine e-mail to all the potential bidders for a bankrupt client. The identities of all these bidders were to be kept secret, but the sender inadvertently included the e-mail addresses of all the potential bidders in the "to" line of the message.[7] That's why I recommend that you think and pause. Then think again.

And what about tone? Because you can't really retrieve a sent e-mail, you ought to be careful with tone. The idea here is to avoid writing to your boss or an important client in the same way you'd write to a colleague or friend. Plus, you want to be careful not to hastily include insensitive statements, private information, or embarrassing mistakes—which of course can be easily forwarded to

---

7. Simon Romero & Geraldine Fabrikant, *Secret List of Potential Suitors Exposed*, New York Times, C2 (April 10, 2002).

hundreds of people. Whenever you're writing an e-mail in your capacity as a lawyer, think of it as a letter. Ask yourself these questions:

- Is this the same tone I would use in a letter?
- Have I edited as carefully as I would a letter?
- Is the content okay to send to this person *and anyone this person forwards to*?

Of course, when you're writing to a friend or colleague about personal matters, it's different. But when you're writing as a lawyer, think of the e-mail message as a letter, not as a note.

Send a clear message in every part of the e-mail.

Make the subject line an effective part of your e-mail messages. Be specific in the subject line—it will often be the sole basis on which someone decides to read or delete your message. Describe what you're writing about as briefly as you can, and think of the subject line as summarizing the message rather than merely defining the topic. Instead of "Discovery matters," write "Approaching discovery deadlines in Henderson case."[8]

To speed things up for your readers, try this tip from law-practice advisor Bill Jawitz. Start the subject with a single word that identifies the purpose of the message:

- Action: (you're giving instructions or an assignment)
- Request: (you're asking the recipient to get back to you)
- Info: (you're giving information, but you don't need a reply)
- Confirmed: (you're letting someone know you understand a request)
- Delivery: (you're providing something requested of you)[9]

Think about changing the subject line if it will help the reader. We've all seen e-mail messages that are replies to replies to some orig-

8. Watkins, *Leave Your Smileys at School* at 25–26.
9. Bill Jawitz, *Best Email Practices for Lawyers*, Success Track Esq, http://www.successtrackesq.com/part-one-of-best-email-practices-for-lawyers/.

inal message that is long forgotten, yet the subject line still says what the original sender wrote. It can be confusing. In an email thread, if the subject matter has actually changed, modify the subject line. You'll be tempted to click "reply," type a short message, and send it. Likewise, you might be inclined to click "forward" and send without thinking. But remember that when you click "reply" or "forward," the subject line does not change. Are you really writing on the same subject? Think. If not, change the subject so it reflects what you're writing about.

3. Frontload your content.

Most legal writing should not be background and then point, but point and then background. Yet many legal writers give background first and then come to the point. For e-mail (and for most legal writing), state the point first and then provide the background. For e-mail, here are two concrete recommendations.

Put questions up front.

If you're asking a question in the message, ask it first. If the reader needs background to understand the question, ask the question and move quickly to the background. In other words, don't do this:

> Don,
>
> I've received a summary judgment motion from the defendant in the Henderson case, but I'm tied up with another matter. It's essentially the same cause of action as the one you worked on in the Kleinsmith case. Kate Landers said you might have some time to put something together for me. Can you prepare a response?

Instead, do this:

> Don,
>
> Can you prepare a response to a summary judgment motion in the Henderson case?

Background: I've received a summary judgment motion from the defendant, but I'm tied up with another matter. It's essentially the same cause of action as the one you worked on in the Kleinsmith case. Kate Landers said you might have some time to put something together for me. Please let me know.

If you ask the question up front, you're more likely to get an answer.

Put answers and conclusions up front.

In a law office today, we frequently transmit the results of legal research—legal analysis and legal conclusions—by e-mail. When you write this kind of e-mail, remember the busy, impatient e-mail reader, and aim to deliver the answer or conclusion as early as possible. In fact, I've begun recommending that writers give the answer to a legal question in the subject line and again in the first paragraph of the body text.

Here's an example, with the up-front answers in boldface type:

From: Chris Smith

To: Miranda Cathcart

Subject: **Answer: Radford cannot prove voluntary renunciation**

Miranda,

You asked if Todd Radford will be able to prove the defense of voluntary renunciation to a charge of attempted kidnapping. **No, Radford will not be able to prove he voluntarily renounced the attempted kidnapping.**

Radford's returning of the boy to the mother coincided almost perfectly with the mother's re-appearance and yelling and also with Radford's seeing her dialing her phone. Even if he had an internal "change of heart" and testified to that change, when the renunciation of an attempt coincides in time with events that make the crime more difficult, courts and juries invariably infer that the events motivated the re-nunciation — so the renunciation is not voluntary.

* * *

An e-mail message reporting the results of research and analysis serves its function best when you frontload the point: the answer to the question or the conclusion you predict.

Chapter 5

Writing to the Client

- *Avoid legalisms.*
- *Limit citations.*
- *Be conversational.*

We all write letters and e-mails to nonlawyer clients at some time. Yet what we write is often poorly targeted to that audience. A partner in a prestigious law firm recently told me he is "appalled" at the writing style of letters his colleagues send to clients: the tone and style are too stuffy and legalistic.

As lawyers, we need to be aware that when we write to clients, we face a dramatic shift in audience. When lawyers write to lawyers, we tend to value specificity and precision above all. What's more, we're accustomed to using insider language when writing to other lawyers, so readability and clarity often take a back seat. But when we write to nonlawyer clients, we need to be sure the big picture gets across clearly, first.

Plus, we can't assume our clients know the legal language; instead, we should use common terms. We shouldn't clutter our prose with ungainly legal citations; rather, we should present the necessary authority in a sensible and streamlined way. And we'd be wise to avoid elevated diction or overly formal language; we should write in a way that is easy to understand.

In this chapter I address three typical characteristics of legal language that appear too often in client letters: legalisms, legal citation, and over-formality. I believe that when we're writing to clients, we ought to limit all three. Doing so is a sign of professional maturity and experience. I'll paraphrase George Bernard Shaw (who used *literature* and *literary* where I'm using *law* and *legal*):

- In law the ambition of a novice is to acquire the legal language; the struggle of the adept is to get rid of it.[1]

1. Avoid legalisms.

Legalisms, according to John Trimble, are "the circumlocutions, formal words, and archaisms that characterize lawyers' speech and writing."[2] They're the lawyer's way of saying something, the musty and legal-sounding words and phrases. They are the distinctive characteristics of traditional legal-writing style.

But you ought to banish them from client letters. Simply put, don't use traditional legal-writing style when writing to clients. Instead, drop the legal words and the archaisms. In essence, try *not* to sound like a lawyer.

That's a challenging standard to meet because legalisms abound in what lawyers read and in what we normally write. Thus, many lawyers will continue to use legalistic words and phrases when writing to clients, primarily for two reasons.

First, some lawyers use legalisms to impress or intimidate the client. Under this theory, the client who is baffled by the language is the client who needs the lawyer. I've had more than a few lawyers propose this theory as a justification for legalese. But the client may also resent the lawyer and look for one who can explain things clearly. I say impress the client with your knowledge of the law, with your ability to get favorable results, and with your hard work. Don't try to impress clients with legalistic language.

Second, some lawyers use legalisms out of habit or reflex. This is understandable. Experienced lawyers have been at it for many years; they're often immersed in their fields, naturally and comfortably at home with the legal language. Or sometimes lawyers forget what they

---

1. Quoted in John R. Trimble, *Writing With Style: Conversations on the Art of Writing* 64 (3d ed., Prentice Hall 2011).
2. Bryan A. Garner, *Garner's Dictionary of Legal Usage* 531 (3d ed., Oxford U. Press 2011).

didn't know. That happens to teachers all the time. You teach the concept from the perspective of one with 10 or 20 years' experience, forgetting that your audience has no experience. But skilled teachers—and lawyers—adapt their teaching and writing to the audience. So when the audience is a nonlawyer client, cut the legalisms.

Here is an example of how to do it.

Examples of legalisms

Read this excerpt from a practitioner's letter to a new client. Typical legalisms are in boldface type.

> Dear Mr. Wilkins:
>
> Enclosed please find the retainer agreement. Please sign and return **same** at your earliest convenience.
>
> **Pursuant to** our conversation of December 20, 2001, I have conducted legal research on the question as to whether your arbitration claim was timely under the Texas Seed Arbitration Act. Tex. Agric. Code Ann. § 64.006(a) (Vernon 2001) (the "Act"). According to Texas **common law** construing the Act, the court would apply the plain-meaning **canon of construction**, *Fitzgerald v. Advanced Germination Systems, Inc.*, 996 S.W.2d 864, 865 (Tex. 1999), and should hold that **said** claim was timely.
>
> Unfortunately, this conclusion is not guaranteed and is subject to certain qualifications discussed **herein**. *See, e.g., Continental Cas. Ins. Co. v. Functional Restoration Assocs.*, 19 S.W.3d 393, 399 (Tex. 2000).

The boldface terms are almost exclusively "legal"; that is, only lawyers use them. These words and phrases fall into different categories: *same, pursuant to, said,* and *herein* are commonly used by lawyers, but do not have unique legal meanings; *common law* and *canon of construction* do have specialized legal meanings. But you can replace all of them with common terms:

Instead of	Write
same	it, the agreement
pursuant to	as discussed in, as we agreed
common law	court cases, judicial decisions
cannon of construction	rule, method of interpreting statutes
said	the, your
herein	here, in this letter

By removing the legalisms, you make the text easier for the client to understand, and you avoid sounding pompous.

2. Limit citations.

The example letter I excerpted contains three legal citations. All three use correct form. All three direct the reader to the proper authority. All three state the proposition they're cited for. So what's the problem?

First, they clutter the text. Although legal readers are used to citations and, frankly, are apt to skip over them, to the uninitiated, they're large road humps. They're too long to be ignored, yet they're not textual sentences, so readers must slow down and try to figure them out. Good client writing doesn't ask the reader to slow down and figure things out.

Second, they contain specialized information that most clients won't understand. In particular, the volume-reporter-page portion of the citation can be baffling: 996 S.W.2d 864. Certainly that means nothing to the nonlawyer client.

Third, citation signals must certainly seem strange to the client. What is *See, e.g.*? Signals are a perfect example of a convention of legal writing with a specialized purpose and meaning. The meaning is not intuitive, but is specially defined in citation manuals. We shouldn't expect our clients to consult a citation manual.

So rather than clog your client letters with legal citations, choose one of these options:

Option A: Omit citation to legal authority altogether.

Ask yourself these questions: How important is it for my client to have the citation to the Texas Agriculture Code? Can't I just say *Texas law* or *Texas statutes*? Does my client need to know that the case I am relying on is *Fitzgerald v. Advanced Germination Systems, Inc.*, that it is found in volume 996 of the *South Western Reporter, Second Series*, page 864, and that it was decided by the Texas Supreme Court in 1999? Besides, is my client going to know what the *South Western Reporter, Second Series* is? Or that it's abbreviated S.W.2d?

Completely omitting the citations in client letters cleans up the text and makes the document much more readable. But some lawyers won't want to go that far. And in some situations, you *will* want the client to know the names and sources of the authority.

Option B: Put the citations in footnotes.

This technique has much the same effect as omitting the citations because now the long, baffling road humps are gone, and the client can read the text smoothly. Most clients will treat the footnotes as "legal stuff" and will ignore them, and those who want the bibliographic information can find it in the footnotes. But footnotes are a mixed blessing. Some clients will be annoyed that some information is at the bottom of the page and requires them to nod up and down to take it all in.

In court papers, footnoting citations is a legitimate practice among lawyers and is recommended by at least one noted expert, Bryan Garner.[3] The practice has detractors, including Judge Richard Posner,

---

3. Bryan A. Garner, *Legal Writing in Plain English: A Text With Exercises* 77–81 (U. Chicago Press 2001).

who primarily focus on the need to consult the page-bottom to see the sources.[4] But for the nonlawyer client—whose need to know the source of authority is much less than a judge's—footnoting the citations can be a good compromise.

Option C: Use a shorthand form to refer to the authority.

Rather than list the entire case name and bibliographic information, simply refer to the case in a shorthand way. Leave the details in a memo to the file. Under Option C, our letter excerpt might look like this (with the legalisms replaced):

Dear Mr. Wilkins:

Enclosed please find the retainer agreement. Please sign and return it at your earliest convenience.

As we discussed in our conversation of December 20, 2001, I have conducted legal research on the question as to whether your arbitration claim was timely under the Texas Seed Arbitration Act. According to the *Fitzgerald* case, the court would apply the plain-meaning rule and should hold that your claim was timely.

Unfortunately, this conclusion is not guaranteed and is subject to certain qualifications discussed in this letter. For example, one qualification arises from a Texas Supreme Court case called *Continental Casualty*, decided in 2000.

This letter is cleaner and clearer, with the clogging citations removed and the legalistic tone pared down. It's much more inviting to a client than the original letter.

---

4. Richard A. Posner, *Against Footnotes*, 38 Court Review: J. Am. Judges Assn. 24 (Summer 2001).

3. Be conversational.

By "conversational," I don't mean you can use slangy or substandard language. I mean "colloquial," another word that should have no pejorative connotations. Rather, to say that someone writes conversationally or colloquially is a compliment: it means writing that is natural and readable. Of course, we should usually not write to clients in the same way we speak or carry on conversation. That's too informal and would appear unprofessional. But we *can* write in a clear, simple, and direct way that avoids pompous, turgid prose.

Ultimately, lawyers should reduce the level of formality when writing to clients. What's too formal and what's too informal is often a matter of taste, but consider a few examples from our revised excerpt. I've highlighted the words and phrases that strike me as unnecessarily formal or stuffy.

> Dear Mr. Wilkins:
>
> **Enclosed please find** the retainer agreement. Please sign and return it **at your earliest convenience.**
>
> As we discussed in our conversation of December 20, 2001, I have **conducted legal research** on **the question as to whether** your arbitration claim was timely under the Texas Seed Arbitration Act. According to a Texas case called *Fitzgerald*, the court would apply the plain-meaning rule and should hold that your claim was **timely**.
>
> **Unfortunately,** this conclusion is not guaranteed and is **subject to certain qualifications** discussed in this letter. For example, one qualification arises from a Texas Supreme Court case called *Continental Casualty* decided in 2000.

None of these words or phrases is wrong or bad; they simply elevate the formality unnecessarily. They create a distance between the writer and the reader—a distance you don't want between you and your client.

Here are some possible revisions:

Formal phrase	Comment
enclosed please find	This phrase and its sibling, *please find enclosed*, have been criticized since 1880.[5] Try *Here is* or *I have enclosed*.
at your earliest convenience	Almost harmless, but stuffy. Try *as soon as you can* or *when you can*.
conducted legal research	One word, *researched*, is turned into three.
the question as to whether	A common legal space-filler. Prefer *whether*.
unfortunately	Perfectly correct, but long. Short transition words make your writing easier to read. Use *but*. And yes, you can start a sentence with *but*.[6]
timely	Harmless. On the other hand, I'd never used the word *timely* until I went to law school. How about *on time*?
subject to certain qualifications	Highly formal. Perhaps we should omit it or revise it in a complete reworking of the sentence. Suggestion: *there are exceptions*.

By avoiding legalisms, limiting citations, and adopting a conversational tone, we now have a shorter, clearer, and more understandable letter. Here's our final revision:

Dear Mr. Wilkins:

Here is the retainer agreement. Please sign and return it as soon as you can.

As we discussed in our conversation of December 20, 2001, I have researched whether your arbitration claim was on time

---

5. Garner, *Garner's Dictionary of Legal Usage*, at 316.
6. Bryan A. Garner, *On Beginning Sentences with But*, Mich. B.J. 43 (Oct. 2003).

under the Texas Seed Arbitration Act. According to the *Fitzgerald* case, the court would apply the plain-meaning rule and should hold that your claim was on time.

But this conclusion is not guaranteed; there are some exceptions, which I discuss in this letter. For example, one exception arises from a Texas Supreme Court case called *Continental Casualty*, decided in 2000.

This version meets and probably exceeds the client-reader's expectations—a legal letter that is conversational and yet professional. This is the kind of letter a client is likely to read and understand.

Chapter 6

Writing to Opposing Counsel

- *Don't antagonize.*
- *Be specific.*
- *Think ahead.*

Just about every lawyer has occasion to write to counsel on the other side of a matter, whether it's a loan deal, a public-utilities rate negotiation, or a lawsuit. In fact, trial lawyers probably do it so frequently it can become mindlessly routine. But we ought to take seriously our communication with opposing counsel—especially our written communication.

After all, in a letter to opposing counsel, you reveal much of yourself: your attitude, your experience, your knowledge, your professionalism. If your letter contains typographical errors, opposing counsel might assume you're sloppy. If your letter contains comma errors, opposing counsel might think you're semi-literate. If your letter contains faulty legal citation, opposing counsel might consider you inept.

Of course, you don't want opposing counsel to think any of those things. So take care when writing to opposing counsel. The tips in this chapter will help.

But first, may I put in a pitch for civility? Try to rise above the petty insults, sarcasm, and mean-spiritedness that appear in some legal correspondence. Did you know the American Bar Association agrees with me? The ABA Section on Litigation has *Guidelines for Conduct* that it adopted in 1996, and they contain the following:

Lawyer's Duties to Other Counsel

1. We will practice our profession with a continuing awareness that our role is to zealously advance the legitimate interests of our clients. In our dealings with others we will not reflect the ill

feelings of our clients. We will treat all other counsel, parties, and witnesses in a civil and courteous manner, not only in court, but also in all other written and oral communications.[1]

What the ABA and I are trying to tell you is to strive for a tone that is assertive without being offensive, firm without being unpleasant, and precise without being insulting. Those are the hallmarks of a professional.

Now to the three specific techniques. (Note: This chapter is designed to improve the letters lawyers write to opposing counsel in any situation, but the suggestions are especially useful for trial practice.)

1. Don't antagonize.

When your client has a problem and feels cheated or taken advantage of, is it your instinct to put on your bulletproof vest and prepare for war? And does your gear include a laptop computer, so you can fire off a nasty letter?

Sometimes your client will want a fight, and you'll agree. Most trial lawyers can provoke one. But what if your client has different expectations? Or what if the fight your client wants is a bad legal move? As Steven Stark, an experienced litigator and author of *Writing to Win*, has said: "[I]t is far more difficult to de-escalate a fight than it is to escalate one."[2] So write that first letter carefully; don't unintentionally antagonize your opponent.

In a recent survey I conducted, I sent sample letters to a dozen practicing attorneys in several fields and with a broad range of experience. I asked them to comment on the letters, specifically on the tone. Their thoughts and suggestions formed the basis of my recommendations here.

To get an idea of what kind of language and tone can antagonize a lawyer, let's study two samples I used in my survey. The first is a letter sent by a plaintiff's lawyer to a defense lawyer representing a potentially opposing party. Let me set the stage.

---

1. ABA, Section of Litigation Guidelines for Conduct (1996).
2. Steven D. Stark, *Writing to Win: The Legal Writer* 256 (2d ed., Three Rivers Press 2012).

Plaintiff's counsel's perspective.

Your client, Adam Ristov, leased a commercial property to a fast-food franchisee. Under the lease, Ristov receives rent plus a percentage of the restaurant's profits. In addition, Ristov says the franchisee had promised him free home delivery of food from the restaurant. But Ristov now says the franchisee refuses to continue home delivery. Ristov and the franchisee have discussed the subject already, but this is the first time a lawyer has gotten involved. Ristov is angry, but what he really wants is to get the home delivery started again without much conflict or cost.

And by the way, you haven't had much time to investigate the underlying details.

How will you phrase your letter? What's the right tone to achieve your client's goals? Here's one possible "first letter," adapted from a real letter. As you read it, ask yourself if the boldface phrases are likely to help or hurt your client's cause.

Dear Ms. Richards:

I represent Adam Ristov, who, as you know, leased a property to your client, Roger Page, in December 2008. Mr. Page **perpetrated a fraud** on Mr. Ristov in connection with the lease and in his subsequent dealings with my client. That fraud needs to be remedied; **to assure a prompt resolution, I am forwarding a copy of this letter to Mr. Page's franchisor,** BurgerTime Restaurants, Inc.

When the property was leased to Mr. Page, he made certain promises about home delivery to Mr. Ristov. I believe the **franchisor ought to know that Mr. Page created this web of lies** merely to induce Mr. Ristov to enter the lease.

As you are obviously aware, Mr. Ristov is entitled to receive a percentage of the restaurant's profits. When my client recently tried to query Mr. Page about the **rash decision** to stop all home delivery, Mr. Page guaranteed that stopping home delivery would increase profits. He thereby **tried to buy off Mr. Ristov.**

* * *

Many lawyers will find nothing wrong with this letter. In fact, about half the lawyers I surveyed say letters like this are fine. On the other hand, that means about half object to letters adopting this antagonistic tone.

I, too, assert that when viewed in context, the boldface phrases would be better revised or omitted. Here are the phrases with my comments:

Problem phrase	Comment
perpetrated a fraud	This phrase directly accuses the opposing counsel's client of fraud. That is a strong accusation and shouldn't be made in the first letter you send to opposing counsel. Besides, it seems premature when you haven't had much time to gather facts.
to assure a prompt resolution, I am forwarding a copy … to Mr. Page's franchisor	In a first letter, this is a drastic step. Sure, you might hope that you will get a better or faster response by copying the higher authority, but you're also likely to get an angrier and more defensive response.
Mr. Page created this web of lies	"Web of lies," besides being a cliché, which you should avoid, unnecessarily characterizes the opposing party negatively. Generally, that's not wise unless you intend to antagonize opposing counsel.
as you are obviously aware	This phrase implies that you can read the mind of opposing counsel and you know what she is aware of. This approach is offensive to some ("how does he know what I'm aware of?") And the tone it sets is somewhat sarcastic.
rash decision	Again, before you've had much time to gather facts, you risk offending unnecessarily by characterizing the opposing party's actions so negatively.
tried to buy off Mr. Ristov	This characterizes the opposing party's actions again. It's a fairly sordid accusation.

Now, how can you improve this letter—for the purposes of getting what your client wants? I offer the following revisions, with explanations:

Problem phrase	Revision	Explanation
perpetrated a fraud	*broke a promise*	In the context, this is probably a more accurate statement. Plus, it doesn't carry the slur of a fraud accusation, yet it still states a basis for legal action.
to assure a prompt resolution, I am forwarding a copy ... to Mr. Page's franchisor	omit	In the first letter, this is better omitted. You might eventually decide to speak to the franchisor, but you'll reduce a lot of tension here if you drop this phrase.
franchisor ought to know that Mr. Page has created this web of lies	*Mr. Ristov relied on Mr. Page's promise of home delivery when Mr. Ristov entered the lease.*	This more concretely describes what happened and omits the antagonizing threat of reporting to the franchisor and the "web of lies" cliché.
as you are obviously aware	*As you may know* or *the lease provides that*	Tone down the assertion of what opposing counsel is aware of, or just state the facts.
rash decision	*decision*	Avoid characterizing the decision.
tried to buy off Mr. Ristov	*effort to dissuade Mr. Ristov was unsuccessful*	Again, rather than commenting on the actions, describe them objectively.

A theme emerges from these revisions: report on what happened instead of commenting on it, characterizing it, or "mind-reading" the motives behind it. This "no mind-reading" approach to legal writing works well in almost any context, but especially here.

Let me emphasize again that our hypothetical client is most concerned with peacefully getting home delivery back. He probably doesn't want to start nasty litigation. If the client does, then the original letter might be just fine.

As a matter of fact, in reviewing the comments of the practicing lawyers I surveyed about this letter, I learned that nearly all believe there's a place for the "nasty" letter. Most said the original letter here is less harsh than others they've seen. So I want to reiterate that you might decide it's appropriate to send a letter exactly like the original. But remember to consider the audience, the goals of your client, and the reaction you might provoke.

Here's a complete revision of the letter for tone:

Dear Ms. Richards:

I represent Adam Ristov, who, as you know, leased a property to your client, Roger Page, in December 2008. Mr. Page broke a promise to Mr. Ristov in connection with the lease and in his subsequent dealings with my client. That needs to be remedied.

When the property was leased to Mr. Page, he made certain promises about home delivery to Mr. Ristov. Mr. Ristov relied on Mr. Page's promise of home delivery when Mr. Ristov entered the lease.

Mr. Ristov is entitled to receive a percentage of the restaurant's profits. When my client recently tried to query Mr. Page about the decision to stop all home delivery, Mr. Page guaranteed that stopping home delivery would increase profits. His effort to dissuade Mr. Ristov was not successful.

* * *

The tone here is more balanced and professional. That's what you should strive for in this kind of letter. Now let's look at the same dispute from the other side.

Defense counsel's perspective.

You've just received a letter that accuses your client of several bad acts. You are writing a response. Your client, a fast-food franchisee, generally likes to take a firm stand so as not to seem like an easy mark for the sue-happy. But your client also wants to avoid nasty litigation — he believes he has spent too much money in the past on lawyers exchanging accusations.

How will you phrase the response? What's the proper tone to achieve your client's goals? The letter below is one possibility, responding to the original version of the plaintiff's letter we discussed. Again, as you read it, ask yourself if the highlighted phrases are likely to help or hurt your client's cause.

Dear Mr. Anderson:

> I am in receipt of your letter dated December 7, 2009, accusing Mr. Page of fraud. These are very serious allegations, and I sincerely hope Mr. Ristov is aware of the damage such **smear tactics** can have, especially when a letter such as yours is sent to a franchisee's franchisor. To try to force Mr. Page into making imprudent business decisions by the **use of defamation** and the **obvious attempt to ruin his reputation** is unconscionable, and very possibly actionable.
>
> **Mr. Page is in the restaurant business to make a profit.** Be assured that any decisions that he has made regarding the Davenport Highway location have been reasonable and are intended to increase the profitability of the restaurant. In addition, Mr. Page certainly did not guarantee increased sales; rather, he simply assured your client that the restaurant would be operated in a profitable manner consistent with his high standards.

* * *

Here are my comments on the highlighted phrases:

Problem phrase	Comments
smear tactics	Besides being a cliché, the phrase implies that you know the opposing counsel's intentions: opposing counsel did not have a legitimate concern but was attempting only to smear your client. The phrase serves only to antagonize.
use of defamation	You object to your client's being accused of fraud, but you now accuse the opposing client of defamation. Hope of cooperation and amicable resolution is fading.
obvious attempt to ruin his reputation	Again, you're reading the mind of opposing counsel and concluding that his intentions are bad. And think hard any time you're tempted to write that something is "obvious."
Mr. Page is in the restaurant business to make a profit	This may sound harmless at first, but it's sarcastic at a minimum and insulting at worst.

To improve this letter, I offer the following revisions:

Problem phrase	Revision	Explanation
smear tactics	*a fraud accusation*	This reports what opposing counsel did without the antagonizing commentary.
use of defamation	*telling his franchisor that he is committing fraud*	Again, this reports what opposing counsel did without accusing him.
obvious attempt to ruin his reputation	*assailing his reputation*	Once again, report what opposing counsel did without negative commentary.
Mr. Page is in ... business to make a profit	*he did not make any business decisions intended to harm your client*	This is what the original implied, but the tone is now direct and not sarcastic.

Here's a revision of the letter for tone:

Dear Mr. Anderson:

I am in receipt of your letter dated December 7, 2009, accusing Mr. Page of fraud. These are very serious allegations, and I sincerely hope Mr. Ristov is aware of the damage a fraud accusation can have, especially when a letter such as yours is sent to a franchisee's franchisor. To try to force Mr. Page into making imprudent business decisions by telling his franchisor he is committing fraud, or by assailing his reputation, is unconscionable and very possibly actionable.

Mr. Page did not make any business decisions intended to harm your client. Rather, be assured that any decisions he made regarding the Davenport Highway location have been reasonable and are intended to increase the profitability of the restaurant. In addition, Mr. Page did not guarantee increased sales; rather, he simply assured your client that the restaurant would be operated in a reasonable manner consistent with his high standards.

* * *

The letter is now more professional and appropriately respectful.

2. Be specific.

When writing to opposing counsel, be as specific and clear as you can within your role. You can't reveal client confidences or release strategic information, but you can explain exactly what happened, what it means, and what you want.

For example, instead of writing, "a breach has occurred," describe the underlying facts, like this: "Your client did not make the December payment, which breaches the contract." Being specific in this way will also help you as you try to avoid antagonizing. Describing something specifically will often keep you from characterizing it or commenting on it.

If the goal is to move the dispute along amicably and to resolve it efficiently for your client, then specificity pays. Specific details in demand letters are easier for opposing counsel to respond to and can speed up and smooth out the resolution of disputes. Likewise, specific responses and explanations when replying to demands are also much more helpful in settling matters than are broad generalizations or vague descriptions.

What's more, if you force yourself to be specific, you'll be less likely to write the reflex-driven "go to war" letter that can so often provoke unnecessary delay, expense, and stress for your client.

Plaintiff's counsel's perspective.

Here's our plaintiff's letter again, with the tone revisions from section one and now with the vague and general phrases in boldface:

Dear Ms. Richards:

I represent Adam Ristov, who, as you know, leased **a property** to your client, Roger Page, in December 1998. Mr. Page broke a promise to Mr. Ristov **in connection with the lease** and in his **subsequent dealings** with my client. That needs to be **remedied.**

When the property was leased to Mr. Page, he made **certain promises about home delivery** to Mr. Ristov. Mr. Ristov relied on Mr. Page's promise of home delivery when Mr. Ristov entered the lease.

The lease provides that Mr. Ristov is entitled to receive a percentage of the restaurant's profits. When my client recently **tried to query Mr. Page about the decision** to stop all home delivery, Mr. Page guaranteed that stopping home delivery would increase profits. His effort to dissuade Mr. Ristov was not successful.

* * *

Now that I've highlighted the nonspecific words and phrases, don't they strike you more strongly as vague and general? What property? What were the subsequent dealings? How, exactly, should the problem be remedied? What were the certain promises? Finally, the "in connection with the lease" phrase and the "tried to query" phrases are unnecessarily vague.

To improve this letter, revise it so it could stand alone—without an explanation from the author. Rather than rely on inside knowledge, which only the author and the client may have, write in a concrete, detailed way so the letter makes sense even to someone not familiar with the situation.

To set up a more specific letter, let's first assume that the "property" has an address. Let's assume that the "subsequent dealings" were continued promises of free home delivery. The remedy we seek is reinstatement of the home delivery. As for the "certain promises" phrase, let's assume it was just careless writing and that it refers to the same promise of home delivery. Finally, let's tighten up the language in the "query" phrase.

Our revised letter might look like this:

Dear Ms. Richards:

I represent Adam Ristov, who, as you know, leased 1285 Davenport Highway to your client, Roger Page, in December 2008. Mr. Page broke a promise to Mr. Ristov. When Mr. Ristov agreed to lease the property to Mr. Page, Page promised the restaurant would be providing home delivery and that Mr. Ristov would get home delivery free. Even later, Page reiterated those promises. But all home delivery has been stopped.

Mr. Ristov relied on Mr. Page's promise of home delivery when Mr. Ristov entered the lease. We therefore insist that home delivery be reinstated, including free delivery to Mr. Ristov.

The lease provides that Mr. Ristov is entitled to receive a percentage of the restaurant's profits. When Mr. Ristov recently asked Mr. Page why he stopped all home delivery, Mr. Page guaranteed that stopping home delivery would increase profits. His effort to dissuade Mr. Ristov was not successful.

* * *

With these revisions, the letter is much clearer and easier to understand.

Defense counsel's perspective.

From the other side, here's the letter with the tone revisions included and the nonspecific phrases highlighted:

Dear Mr. Anderson:

I am in receipt of your letter dated December 7, 2009, accusing Mr. Page of **fraud**. These are very serious allegations, and I sincerely hope Mr. Ristov is aware of **the damage** a fraud accusation can have, especially when a letter such as yours is sent to a franchisee's franchisor. To try to force Mr. Page into **making imprudent business decisions** by telling his franchisor he is committing fraud, or by **assailing his reputation**, is unconscionable and very possibly actionable.

Mr. Page did not make any business decisions intended to harm your client. Rather, be assured that **any decisions he made** regarding the Davenport Highway location have been reasonable and are intended to increase the profitability of the restaurant. In addition, Mr. Page did not guarantee increased sales; rather, he simply assured that the restaurant would be operated in a reasonable manner consistent with his high standards.

* * *

As before, you'll notice the letter is fairly vague. What were the fraud accusations? What kind of damage could they cause? How was Mr. Page's reputation assailed? And what are these imprudent business decisions?

Again, revise it so it could be read alone—without the context of the letter it is responding to. Rather than rely on the content of the first letter and simply refer to it, restate the details—briefly—so your letter makes sense even if read in isolation. Ideally, write it so someone who hasn't read the first letter can still understand it.

Here's an attempt at adding concreteness to the letter:

Dear Mr. Anderson:

I am in receipt of your letter dated December 7, 1999, accusing Mr. Page of breaking a promise about home delivery. These are very serious allegations, and I sincerely hope Mr. Ristov is aware that accusing a franchisee of deceit could cause the franchisee to lose the franchise, especially when the accusation is reported to the franchisor. To try to force Mr. Page into continuing home delivery—when it is not profitable—by telling his franchisor he is dishonest is unconscionable and very possibly actionable.

Mr. Page did not make any business decisions intended to harm your client. Rather, be assured that his decision to stop all home delivery at the Davenport Highway location was reasonable and was intended to increase the profitability of the restaurant. In addition, Mr. Page did not guarantee increased sales; rather, he simply assured that the restaurant would be operated in a reasonable manner consistent with his high standards.

* * *

Thus, an evenhanded tone and careful, specific writing can improve any letter directed to opposing counsel. But tone and specificity are not enough; foresight is vital.

3. Think ahead.

An experienced litigator once gave me this advice, which I think is valuable enough to highlight here:

- Whenever you write a letter to opposing counsel in litigation, treat it as though you'll see it again—in court.

A colleague put it to me this way:

- Before you send any letter, imagine it enlarged as a trial exhibit.

That's good advice, and memorable, too. The reminder to think ahead when writing to opposing counsel comes down to three things, and here are some suggestions related to our fast-food franchise letter:

1. *Think ahead to future disputes, future problems, and future actions.*

- Anticipate what might happen and write with that in mind. Is this dispute over the stopping of home delivery going to become a lawsuit? Or is it a small matter that will go away soon? Or is it just a small piece of a larger, troubled relationship— are there deeper frustrations and disagreements?

2. *Think ahead to the opposing client's and opposing counsel's reactions.*

- Ask yourself what you would do if you received this letter. Write accordingly. If there's a chance to settle this amicably, will accusing the other side of fraud and rash decisions make them so mad he won't back down?

3. *Think ahead to the judge or jury as they hear your letter being read aloud in court.*

- How will it sound? Will it hurt your case? Will it make you look petty, harsh, or unreasonable? Will the judge or jury be able to see you as a victim, when your first letter contained some fairly nasty accusations?

Ultimately, as you write to opposing counsel, always remember the audience. Avoid writing something you would find provocative because it will certainly provoke the opposing lawyer. If you want to speed up and streamline the process, be as specific as you can. And always anticipate what could happen to your letter and how it could even be used against you.

Chapter 7

Writing to the Mediator

- *Write to learn.*
- *Be brief but not brief-like.*
- *Make information accessible.*

More and more lawyers must participate in alternative dispute resolution every year, and these lawyers are not just litigators. Corporate counsel, government lawyers, and even transactional lawyers will, in a typical career, participate in several disputes that are directed away from a formal trial and toward another form of dispute resolution. Mediation is the most commonly-used form.

For most mediation sessions, you'll have to prepare a mediation statement, sometimes called a pre-mediation submission, a pre-mediation questionnaire, or a written summary of issues. Mediators usually—but not always—require lawyers to submit these written statements before the session. Most use one of two formats: (1) the mediator may give the lawyer a set of questions—sometimes with limited space for answers, or (2) the mediator may ask for a summary of the party's view of the issues and a statement of its position. Generally, these statements are confidential and are for the mediator only. They're not submitted to opposing counsel.

No matter the required format of the mediation statement, it needs to be well written and clear. But how can it be most effective? Follow these tips.

1. Write to learn.

When the mediator requires the parties to submit a mediation statement before the session, the mediator usually has two purposes in mind.[1]

First, the mediator needs to be educated about the dispute. The mediation statement typically informs the mediator about the facts of the case and the issues raised, so the mediator will have some understanding of the case before the mediation session. Otherwise, according to Eric Galton, author of *Representing Clients in Mediation*, and an experienced mediator, valuable time at the session is wasted educating the mediator about the dispute.[2] Expecting the mediator to pick up the information at the session is unwise:

> The parties' time, as well as the mediator's, is better spent advocating positions and moving the discussions toward settlement than going over material for the first time that could easily have been set out in the mediation statement.[3]

Second, the mediator wants the lawyer and the lawyer's client to *learn more about their own case.* As paradoxical as this may seem in light of the first purpose of educating the mediator, it is still true. For the lawyer and the client, preparing the statement is an opportunity to begin a formal evaluation of the case that can help them develop settlement ranges and strategies. Thus, the mediation statement helps the lawyer and client focus on their case in a realistic and thoughtful way. According to Galton: "I want the lawyers to focus on and objectively evaluate their case prior to the session."[4]

The key word here is *objectively.* The parties may have been in litigation for quite a while, and discovery may be completed, but there may have been little time for the lawyers to carefully analyze the case

---

1. My acknowledgments to experienced mediator John Fleming of Austin, Texas, who provided much of the background information here.

2. Eric Galton, *Representing Clients in Mediation* 55 (Am. Law. Media 1994).

3. Maryland Inst. for Continuing Prof. Educ. of Laws., Inc., *Mediation: A Handbook for Maryland Lawyers* Ch. VI (1999).

4. Galton, *Representing Clients in Mediation* at 55.

for purposes of settlement. To settle, you must compromise. To compromise, you must be able to see the other side. To see the other side, you must bring some objectivity to the dispute.

And there's nothing like having to write a summary of your case to force you to think about it in a clear and organized way. So when you're asked to prepare a mediation statement, set yourself to the task knowing ahead of time that the mediator may have an ulterior motive in requiring you to prepare the statement. Be aware you're educating not only the mediator but yourself and your client.

Also, because the mediation statement is confidential and the mediator typically won't show it to opposing counsel, you can be candid and objective in assessing your case. As a result, you may identify weaknesses in your case you hadn't previously discovered, and you'll be able to prepare to defend them. You'll surely identify new strengths in your case, too.

2. Be brief but not brief-like.

Nearly all lawyers are familiar with brief writing; we all probably wrote our first appellate briefs in the first year of law school. Some of us have continued to write briefs—at the trial or appellate level—for our entire careers. But the format, tone, and style of a trial or appellate brief will not be ideal for a mediation statement. You must adapt to the needs of the audience—the mediator.

What most mediators want is a simplified statement of what the parties are stuck on. But mediators, like all legal professionals, are busy. So the simplified statement must also be short. How short? Mediation expert John Fleming says you can accomplish the short, simple statement in "something less than 10 [double-spaced] pages in most cases."[5] That's a challenging task, but well worth the effort because you'll score points with the mediator.

In fact, if your statement is too long, you risk having the mediator skip it: Fleming points out that "Mediators, like judges, are less

---

5. Remarks of John Fleming to the author.

likely to read 70 pages than they are 10 pages." So the mediation statement must be short *and* efficient. You can't waste space. To achieve
those goals, remember two things.

First, avoid formatting your mediation statement like a traditional
trial or appellate brief. For example, unless the mediator requires it,
don't include the standard case caption and style; instead, give the
names of the parties briefly:

Instead of this:

CAUSE NO. 55-5558

REGINALD E. BAKER, Plaintiff,	§ § §	**IN THE DISTRICT COURT** **OF**
	§ §	
v.	§ §	**WRIGHT COUNTY, TEXAS**
	§	
STATE COMMISSION ON **WAGES AND STATE LABOR** **COMMISSION,** Defendant.	§ § §	**555TH JUDICIAL DISTRICT**

PLAINTIFF'S MEDIATION STATEMENT

Try this:

Mediation Statement of Reginald Baker

Plaintiff in
*Reginald Baker v. State Commission on Wages and State
Labor Commission*

Pending in
Wright County, Texas, District Court #555.

Also, avoid using a table of contents (unless your mediation statement is very long, which it should not be). And don't include a table of authorities, a statement of jurisdiction, or any of the other merely procedural parts of a traditional brief. You might want to include a statement of the issues and a statement of facts, but avoid unnecessary clutter and content.

Second, avoid using the advocating tone and persuasive approach of a brief. Remember, the advice here assumes the opposing counsel won't see the mediation statement, so there's no need to phrase everything as positively as possible or to hide all weaknesses. Your mediation statement also should not be admissible in court. So be straightforward and candid. You need not impress the mediator with your persuasive abilities, either. The mediator is not a judge, but instead, Galton states, "must remain neutral and never will rule on a point of law or a disputed fact."[6] As you write the statement, always keep in mind that it is "more important to educate—not to influence—the mediator."[7]

Third, don't cite legal authority in the same way you would in a brief. As noted, mediators do not make rulings or issue findings, much less enter judgments. Of course, there's no harm in pointing out the most important legal authority or a controlling appellate decision. You should. But for that purpose, Galton recommends attaching a short memorandum on the law, with copies of the relevant authorities.[8] Generally, avoid including a detailed legal discussion in your mediation statement.

Ultimately, it's a mistake to prepare a mediation statement that looks and sounds like a brief. It is, however, a mistake many lawyers still make, according to the experts. Many lawyers unfamiliar with mediation believe that the purpose of the mediation statement is to convince the mediator their side is correct. But to write an effective mediation statement, you'll have to let go of that impulse.

---

6. Galton, *Representing Clients in Mediation* at 55.
7. *Mediation: A Handbook for Maryland Lawyers* at Ch. VI.
8. Galton, *Representing Clients in Mediation* at 55.

Besides, if you write a brief-like mediation statement, you send the wrong message. You indirectly tell the mediator that you didn't carefully and objectively assess your own case. Instead, you wrote a persuasive brief designed to convince the mediator of the correctness of your position. Experts in mediation agree that when the statement is written to persuade the mediator, the value of the statement as a tool for case analysis by the lawyer and client is lost.[9] Since that's one reason the mediator asked for the statement in the first place, your brief-like mediation statement tells the mediator that you haven't focused on your case in an objective way.

3. Make information accessible.

We now know the mediation statement is written partly to educate the mediator and partly to educate the author; we also know the statement must be short and efficient. If it truly achieves those ends, it needs only one more attribute to make it superb: accessibility. In her book, *Guide to Legal Writing Style*, Terri LeClercq put it like this:

> Your readers are not going to look at your document because they have extra time or because they need entertainment. Rather, they need information — and fast.[10]

Every important piece of information in the statement ought to be easy to find. You can accomplish that by using three techniques.

Put a summary up front.

This principle has been stressed again and again in this book, but it bears repeating because so many lawyers place the critical information in the middle. If you write an opening statement containing only preliminaries or party introductions or background facts, you're wasting space. Get to the point, as the legal-writing expert Bryan Garner says: "The ideal introduction concisely states the exact points at

---

9. Remarks of John Fleming to the author.

10. Terri LeClercq, *Guide to Legal Writing Style* 97 (2d ed., Aspen L. & Bus. 2000).

issue. Stripped of all extraneous matter, the intro serves as an executive summary: it places the essential ideas before the reader."[11]

So save the factual background for the facts section, and let the title of your document introduce the document. In the first paragraph of your mediation statement, place the "essential ideas" before the mediator. Consider this example.

Original opening paragraph of mediation statement.

FACTUAL BACKGROUND

On June 27, 1997, Baker began employment with the State Commission on Wages (SCW) as Assistant Director of Administrative Services. Baker was subsequently promoted twice while at SCW. Specifically, on June 1, 1998, Baker was promoted to Executive Director for Finance and Administration, and on February 1, 1999, Baker was promoted to Chief Executive and Administrative Officer for SCW. As Chief Executive and Administrative Officer, Baker received a salary of approximately $67,000.

Obviously, this paragraph tells us nothing about the crux of the dispute before the mediator. For this reason, I always advise against *opening* with factual background. Of course, you must give the factual background somewhere, but you don't have to give it first, in the prime location for getting your point across. State the issue and your proposed resolution first, like this:

Revised opening paragraph of mediation statement.

Summary

When the State Commission on Wages was placed in conservatorship, the conservators told Reginald Baker they were going to eliminate the position he held as Chief Executive and Administrative Officer. Evidence now shows they did not eliminate the position. Instead, they hired another person, an employee of one of the conservators with less experience

---

11. Bryan A. Garner, *Legal Writing in Plain English: A Text with Exercises* 55 (U. Chicago Press 2001).

than Baker, as Chief Executive and Administrative Officer. They fired Baker. He seeks damages for wrongful termination.

This paragraph tells the mediator the main point of the dispute and how this party views the issue. It's an efficient and effective summary.

Summarize facts into a narrative.

By the time you're writing the mediation statement, you've probably completed discovery—including depositions. So you ought to know the facts well. But the mediator doesn't, so you must present the facts in an understandable way. In writing about the facts you've discovered, follow these tips.

Avoid telling the story in the order you learned it. It may have come to you in bits and pieces, from depositions and documents. But you must consolidate that information, organize it, and present it in a readable narrative. As much as possible, present a chronological story. Although you might occasionally abandon chronological order to emphasize a point, varying from chronological order is a technique of persuasion that is usually out of place in a mediation statement.

Stories are usually told in chronological order, and stories are memorable. As Terri LeClercq put it, "Chronology's strength is its narrative; of all organizational patterns, a reader is most likely to remember a story."[12]

Also, avoid the all-too-common brief-writing practice of summarizing testimony witness-by-witness. That technique is sure to annoy mediators as much as it annoys judges: Judge Roger J. Miner, of the United States Court of Appeals for the Second Circuit, says that "Some lawyers have the bad habit of presenting the facts by summarizing the testimony of each witness. We much prefer a narrative of the facts."[13]

---

12. Terri LeClercq, *Expert Legal Writing* 104 (U. Tex. Press 1995).
13. Roger J. Miner, *Twenty-Five "Dos" for Appellate Brief Writers*, 3 Scribes J. Leg. Writing 19, 22 (1992).

Design documents with white space and accessible formatting.

Document design and formatting are, on the surface, simple things that might seem unimportant. Or perhaps they seem beneath us as attorneys. Yet recognized experts in legal writing continue to tell us that it matters how our documents look:

- "Failing to use these [document design] options knowledgeably will put you at a disadvantage because readers have become accustomed to well-designed documents."—Bryan Garner in *Garner's Dictionary of Legal Usage*.[14]
- "Modern law offices ... are no longer confined to preprinted forms and typewritten documents.... [L]egal writers now face decisions about formatting virtually every piece of writing produced."—Martha Faulk and Irving Mehler in *The Elements of Legal Writing*.[15]
- "[G]ood document design can encourage readers and make them more efficient in extracting information from a document.... Legal writers who want to give their writing the best chance of being read and understood will pay attention to document design."—Michéle Asprey in *Plain Language for Lawyers*.[16]

The lawyer and document designer Matthew Butterick puts it this way: "Because our writing matters, our typography matters."[17] For a thorough treatment of legal-document format and layout, see his book, *Typography for Lawyers*.

---

14. Bryan A. Garner, *Garner's Dictionary of Legal Usage* 291 (3d ed., Oxford U. Press 2011).

15. Martha Faulk & Irving Mehler, *The Elements of Legal Writing: A Guide to the Principles of Writing Clear, Concise, and Persuasive Legal Documents* 99 (Macmillan 1994).

16. Michéle M. Asprey, *Plain Language for Lawyers* 204 (2d ed., Federation Press 1996).

17. Matthew Butterick, *Typography for Lawyers* 14 (Jones McClure 2010).

For mediation statements, you can use three contemporary techniques for designing a reader-friendly document.

- *White space.* Leave ample space between the sections or parts of the statement. This doesn't mean you must always double-space the text. In fact, if you use ample white space and short paragraphs, single-spaced text will look better and be easier to read. Follow the requirements of the mediator, though. And make sure the left and right margins are at least one inch.

- *Type.* Select a readable type size, probably 12- or 13-point type if you're using Times New Roman — but feel free to use a more modern, readable typeface. (I like Constantia, Cambria, and Garamond.) Never submit a mediation statement in 10-point type or smaller. Be sure to use boldface or another technique to make your headings stand out. But remember moderation and professionalism. Don't get carried away with fancy typefaces or excessive size variations.

- *Graphics.* Use aligned indentations to set off important information. Use bullets to highlight the content of lists. Use text boxes or tables to draw attention to critical information or to make a summary stand out.

In the following excerpt, notice the use of fonts, boldface, bullets, and headings.

Summary

When the State Commission on Wages was placed in conservatorship, the conservators told Reginald Baker they were going to eliminate his position — Chief Executive and Administrative Officer. Evidence now shows they did not eliminate the position. Instead, they hired an employee of one of the conservators — with less experience than Baker — as Chief Executive and Administrative Officer. They fired Baker. He seeks damages for wrongful termination.

Facts

Baker's experience and credentials. Reginald Baker is an experienced administrative-agency supervisor with impressive credentials:

- He has a B.S. in civil engineering from Texas A&M University.
- He has a Master of Public Administration from Louisiana State University.
- He has worked for state agencies for 14 years, with seven years of supervisory experience.

Baker began working at the State Commission on Wages in 1997 as Assistant Director of Administrative Services. He was twice promoted while at the Commission, first to Executive Director for Finance and Administration, and in February 1999 to Chief Executive and Administrative Officer. His salary was $67,000....

Conservatorship. The Commission was placed in conservatorship in 2000. The parties do not dispute that Mr. Baker was not at fault for the causes of the Commission's going into conservatorship....

The conservators hired Rita Harrow as the new Chief Executive and Administrative Officer; she holds a Bachelor of Industrial and Labor Relations from Cornell University and a Masters of Public Administration from the University of Alabama. We acknowledge that her education suits her for the work of Chief Executive and Administrative Officer. But she had not previously worked in a supervisory position at a state agency. She was previously employed at Hardy Technology Systems, owned by one of the conservators, Jake Hardy....

Proposed Dispute Resolution

Mr. Baker believes that the conservators hired a business associate of one of the conservators to replace him but deceived him as to that fact. Their actions caused him to be unemployed for nearly two years and to miss out on career-advancement opportunities. He specifically seeks the following redress:

1. $125,000 in monetary damages.
2. Reinstatement in a supervisory position at the Commission.

This excerpted statement is straightforward, well formatted, and easy to read. It invites the mediator to quickly and easily grasp the key facts and the important issues. And it presents the information without exaggeration and without hiding anything.

Chapter 8

Writing to the Trial Judge

For motions

- *Use a bold synopsis.*
- *Organize overtly.*
- *Be honest.*

For affidavits

- *Use a bold synopsis.*
- *Use headings.*
- *Cut archaic, formulaic language.*

During a career, a trial lawyer will write hundreds—if not thousands—of papers directed to trial judges. Yet so much of what is written for trial judges is not well suited to that audience. Too often, we lawyers treat judges as if they were reading machines—obligated to read what we submit, no matter how difficult that is.

But trial judges, as an audience, are operating under demanding circumstances:

- Trial judges are busy, yet many court papers require them to plow through lengthy preliminaries.
- Trial judges deal with numerous matters, yet many court papers bury the critical point—what separates this case from others—in undifferentiated blocks of text.
- Trial judges must make informed decisions, yet some court papers fudge on the facts or the law or both.

This chapter can't fix all the problems with writing for trial judges, but it offers six suggestions—three for motions and three for affidavits—that will help you get the trial judge's attention, keep it, and deserve it.

For Motions

1. Use a bold synopsis.

Do you begin your court papers by introducing the parties and the procedural background? Stop it. You're squandering a great chance to get your point across. One experienced practitioner and expert writer, Beverly Ray Burlingame, put it this way:

> By devoting the entire opening paragraph to restating the needlessly long title, lawyers waste judges' time and sacrifice a valuable chance for persuasion.[1]

So put a summary of your point or points up front. Giving a summary at the beginning isn't a new idea. Many legal-writing experts recommend it. Here's a sampling of their advice:

> State your conclusion on any specific issue at the outset. — John Dernbach, *et al.*, *A Practical Guide to Legal Writing & Legal Method.*[2]

> In each part of your legal analysis, give the bottom line first. — Irwin Alterman, *Plain & Accurate Style in Court Papers.*[3]

> All filings should have a first-page, introductory summary, whether the rules require one or not. — Steven D. Stark, *Writing to Win.*[4]

So in any court paper, put a summary right at the beginning. Whether you state the issue and answer, summarize your position, or assert the correct result, you should do it up front. Yet too many court papers don't.

---

1. Beverly Ray Burlingame, *On Beginning a Court Paper*, 6 Scribes J. Leg. Writing 160, 161 (1996–1997).

2. John C. Dernbach, Richard V. Singleton II, Cathleen S. Wharton, Joan M. Ruhtenberg, & Catherine J. Wasson, *A Practical Guide to Legal Writing & Legal Method* 215 (4th ed., Aspen Publishers 2010).

3. Irwin Alterman, *Plain & Accurate Style in Court Papers* 97 (ALI-ABA 1987).

4. Steven D. Stark, *Writing to Win: The Legal Writer* 171 (2d ed., Three Rivers Press 2012).

To emphatically implement this advice, I recommend that when you submit a motion to a trial judge, you begin with a bold synopsis, an idea I wrote about in a Texas Bar Journal piece called *The Bold Synopsis: A Way to Improve Your Motions.*[5] It's an excellent way to put a summary right up front. To use it, write a one- to three-sentence summary of your point—what you want and why you should get it, highlight it with boldface text, and set it off with indentations. To see how it works, compare these before-and-after examples of trial motions:

Before—a typical first page

> *DEFENDANTS' MOTION FOR SUMMARY*
> **JUDGMENT & BRIEF IN SUPPORT THEREOF**
> TO THE HONORABLE JUDGE OF SAID COURT:
> COMES NOW CHRIS SMITH AND READY-FOODS, INC., D/B/A ARBY'S, collectively ("Defendants"), pursuant to Rule 166a, and move this Court to grant summary judgment against all claims of Remy Gonzalez ("Plaintiff"), in the above-referenced matter....
>
> * * *

This standard opener tells the judge almost nothing about the issue and nothing specific about the grounds for the motion. It's all background information available elsewhere. Instead, get right to the point; tell the judge the purpose of the motion, specifically, right at the beginning.

After—with a bold synopsis

> Motion for Summary Judgment
> **Chris Smith and Arby's move for summary judgment because they were never the plaintiff's employer under Texas law. In addition, the plaintiff has not exhausted his administrative remedies.**

---

5. Wayne Schiess, *The Bold Synopsis: A Way to Improve Your Motions*, 63 Tex. B.J. 1030 (Dec. 2000).

1. Background....

Here's another before-and-after example. Notice that the writer takes up a good portion of the original opener by defining party names. If that's necessary at all, the first paragraph is not the place to do it. Get the judge focused on your points, not on the parties' defined names:

Before — a typical opener

PLAINTIFF'S TRIAL BRIEF

Plaintiff, Reginald E. Curtis ("Curtis"), files his Trial Brief in his suit against the Texas Commission on Wages ("TCW") and the Texas Labor Commission ("TLC") (collectively, "Defendants"), as follows ...

After — with a bold synopsis

Plaintiff's Trial Brief

The EEOC's conclusions and factual findings should be admitted into evidence here. Its hearings involved the same parties as in this suit, and its conclusions and factual findings are highly probative of discrimination.

1. Background....

Trial judges are busy. The bold synopsis — or any up-front summary — will help the judge by putting the critical information first. That way, the judge does not waste time searching through your document, looking for the point. Judges will appreciate that.

2. Organize overtly.

Now, suppose the judge has the time to read your whole document. How will the judge differentiate your case, your issues, your points, from all the other cases on the docket? The best way to ensure that a trial judge will understand your case is to make the organization of your paper obvious. Make your organizational plan overt.

Section headings

To do that, one good technique is to use short, boldface headings for each new section. By using short, boldface headings, you allow the judge, at any point in the text, to refer to a subject heading and quickly get oriented. Headings are cues to large-scale organization. For example:

Motion in Limine

This motion asks the court to exclude evidence that Regional Hospital fired Nurse Esther Green. The firing was a "subsequent remedial measure" and is inadmissible under Rule 407.

1. Background

This case was filed on ...

2. Authority

Under the Federal Rules of Evidence ...

3. Statement of Facts

Esther Green began working at Regional Hospital ...

4. Argument

Evidence of Nurse Green's dismissal is not admissible ...

The busy judge may want to skip ahead to the critical information, and the headings allow that. The busy judge may forget what's going on in your case, and the headings bring the judge's attention back into focus. In short, the headings make it easy on the judge. And that's good.

Inline headings

You can add another level of headings to a court filing without adding clutter by using inline headings (also called run-in headings). An inline heading is placed in the same line of text as the first line of a paragraph. You can highlight it with boldface, bold italics, or italics. Inline headings are useful to break up a long statement of facts.

3. Statement of Facts

Hiring of Nurse Green. Esther Green began working at Regional Hospital in early January 2011 ...

Improper-dosing event. Nurse Green was assigned to care for Brian Pace, an adult male patient at Regional Hospital ...

Firing of Nurse Green. Regional Hospital fired Esther Green less than a month after the improper-dosing event ...

Enumeration and tabulation

To cue the judge about the small-scale organization and ordering, I recommend breaking up long or complex ideas into smaller chunks of text. Use enumeration (*1, 2, 3* or *a, b, c*) and tabulation (placing text on its own line, using hard returns) to help you organize the text, highlight important material, and cue the judge about the structure—the small-scale organization. In other words, these techniques tell the judge where you are with this idea, as opposed to where you are in this document.

Just to clarify what I mean by enumeration and tabulation, here are some examples:

An example of enumeration:

Legal documents should be (1) lettered, (2) numbered, or (3) tabulated.

An example of tabulation (each item on its own line):

Legal documents should be

lettered,
numbered,   or
tabulated.

An example of tabulation with enumeration:

Legal documents should be

1.   lettered,
2.   numbered, or
3.   tabulated.

Even for something as common as reciting of a rule of law, you can use tabulation to present the rule in a clear and direct way:

Instead of this:

> To decide if the limits on the borrower's selling the property are valid, courts have distinguished between a "direct and total deprivation" of the right to sell, and "mere impingement" of that right. *Spielman-Fond, Inc. v. Hanson's, Inc.*, 379 F. Supp. 997, 999 (D. Ariz. 1973). A direct and total deprivation of the right to sell is more serious. *Id.* It means preventing the sale by seizing the property or by enforcing statutory or contractual terms that prohibit the sale. *Id.* Mere impingement simply means discouraging the sale or making it more difficult. *Id.*

Try this:

> **Rule of Law.** To decide if the limits on the borrower's selling the property are valid, courts have distinguished between:
>
> 1. a "direct and total deprivation" of the right to sell, and
> 2. "mere impingement" of that right.
>
> *Spielman-Fond, Inc. v. Hanson's, Inc.*, 379 F. Supp. 997, 999 (D. Ariz. 1973). A direct and total deprivation of the right to sell is more serious. *Id.* It means preventing the sale by seizing the property or by enforcing statutory or contractual terms that prohibit the sale. *Id.* Mere impingement simply means discouraging the sale or making it more difficult. *Id.*

With traditional headings, inline headings, enumeration, and tabulation, your documents will stand out. Your points will be understandable. Your case will capture the judge's attention.

3. Be honest.

In his excellent book, *Writing to Win: The Legal Writer*, Steven Stark lists "Thirteen Rules of Professionalism in Legal Writing." Here are the first five rules:

1. Never lie, under any circumstance.
2. Don't plagiarize.
3. Don't use euphemisms to disguise the truth.
4. If it's not required, hedging is a form of dishonesty.
5. Avoid the use of hyperbole to distort the truth of your assertions.[6]

Wow. Do you get the impression that Stark, a former judicial clerk and an experienced litigator, is big on honesty? Well trial judges are, too. Consider a quotation on honesty and candor from Judge Stanley Sporkin, formerly of the federal district court in Washington, D.C.

> A lawyer's credibility with the judge ... is the key to any litigation. Candor is essential. Be honest with the judge.... [7]

So in every court paper you submit to a trial judge, be honest.

Be honest about the facts.

Tell the truth about the facts of your case. Don't omit relevant facts, even if they're unfavorable. Don't fudge. And by fudge, I mean to falsify or fake. If you fudge, you risk your credibility. Remember that several potential audiences can scrutinize your court paper besides your colleagues and your own client: the trial judge, the judge's clerk, and — since most court papers are public documents — the press. Someone will figure out that you've fudged on the truth and bring it to the judge's attention.

And don't forget opposing counsel. One experienced litigator reminded me that in a lawsuit, opposing counsel is getting paid to look for your mistakes: "With a paid critic always checking your work, it just doesn't make sense to fudge."[8]

If you do fudge, you'll lose credibility with the judge, and it might mean sanctions or bar discipline. So write about the facts as favorably as possible for your client, but write honestly.

---

6. Stark, *Writing to Win*, at 289.
7. Stanley Sporkin, *The Inside Scoop*, 27 Litigation 3, 3 (Spring 2001).
8. Kamela Bridges, comments to the author.

Be honest about the law.

Sometimes amateurs make mistakes in this area, like the student in this story, who omitted part of the rule of law:

> In the case the students were working on, the rule was that the court should look at five factors to determine the reliability of a witness. Tom chose to discuss only three of the factors and omit the two that hurt his case. [His writing instructor] commented on this problem by writing, "What about the other two factors?" [Tom responded], "Why put them in? They kill my case."[9]

That's a naive mistake by a novice legal writer, and I hope it doesn't sound familiar. You can't afford to make that mistake. Read the cases you cite, report their holdings accurately, and check thoroughly to be sure your cases are still good law.

But why? In Tom's case, the writing instructor had the right response. If you don't report the rule of law accurately, the instructor said, "the State [opposing counsel] will seize on your omission and argue your lack of candor to the court."[10] If you're dishonest about the law, opposing counsel will not let the judge forget it. Judge Sporkin put it this way:

> If you try to spin a court by hiding a key decision that goes against you, the chances are the judge will find out about the decision either from your adversary or from a law clerk. At that point, your credibility is zero.[11]

An up-front summary, an obvious organizational plan, and honesty: three writing skills that will please trial judges—and might even surprise them.

---

9. Anne Enquist, Critiquing Law Students' Writing: What the Students Say Is Effective, 2 J. of Leg. Writing Inst. 145, 165 (1996).

10. *Id.*

11. Stanley Sporkin, *The Inside Scoop*, 27 Litigation 3, 3 (Spring 2001).

For Affidavits

Most lawyers will need to prepare an affidavit at some time; many will write dozens, if not hundreds. So how effectively are you writing them? For most lawyers, writing an affidavit is strictly routine: drag out an old form, duplicate it, and change the details. Done. The result is a formulaic and bland document.

Formulaic and bland is perhaps fine for some affidavits, but many affidavits are important. You might be counting on an affidavit to get a crucial point across to the opposing counsel, the judge, or the hearing examiner. So how can you make your affidavit stand out from the routine and the mundane?

If you want people to read and understand your affidavits quickly and easily, you should apply three simple techniques:

1. Use the bold synopsis.

I've said it throughout this book, but I'll say it again: One of the most important principles in legal writing is to provide an up-front summary. Put the critical information first. I'm reiterating it because it's so often ignored. And affidavits, of all legal documents, are among the worst offenders. Usually, the main point of an affidavit is buried somewhere in the middle of the document. For example, read this affidavit and pay attention to when you know what the critical point is.

AFFIDAVIT

STATE OF TEXAS	§
	§
COUNTY OF TRAVIS	§

DENNIS RAGLEY, being duly sworn, deposes and says:

1.   My name is Dennis Ragley. I am over 21 years of age, of sound mind, and I have personal knowledge of the facts stated herein.

2.   I am the District Supervisor for ReadyFoods, Inc., and I am responsible for 10 restaurants in the south Texas area, including the Beaumont Freddy's restaurant.

3.   On July 10, 1999, I was called by Celia Gonzales, assistant manager at the Beaumont restaurant, and was informed that a shift manager, Kenneth Ivey, had called in and said that he would not work his scheduled shift because his cat had died that morning. In addition, Ivey had not found someone to cover his shift during his absence.

4.   I called Kim Henderson, who was originally scheduled to begin working at the restaurant as the General Manager on July 17, 1999, and asked if she would cover Kenneth Ivey's shift since he had not found anyone to cover his shift.

5.   I also asked Kim Henderson to suspend Kenneth Ivey without pay until I could speak with the company's human resources department concerning proper discipline.

6.   After speaking with Demetria Suka, the human resource administrator, and Ted Whitney, General Counsel for Ready-Foods, Inc., I decided that Kenneth Ivey should be demoted for failing to work his scheduled shift and for failing to find a person to cover his shift. The fact that Kenneth Ivey was a male had absolutely no bearing on my decision to demote Mr. Ivey.

7.   No other employee has ever been given time off for the death of his or her pet.

8. Mr. Ivey was demoted because he had shown by his actions that he could not handle the responsibility of being a shift manager.

9. The foregoing Affidavit consisting of one (1) typewritten page is true and correct.

FURTHER AFFIANT SAYETH NAUGHT

What is the critical information in this affidavit? It is that Mr. Ivey was demoted after he missed work because his cat died and not because he is a male. Now, where did you realize that? Probably in paragraph 6; that's where I grasped the main point of the story—the critical information in the affidavit.

But there's no reason an affidavit must be written that way, with the critical point hiding in paragraph 6. Affidavits, like nearly all legal writing, ought to introduce the main point right up front. You can put the main point up front with a bold synopsis.

I suggest that all affidavits contain a bold synopsis. To create a bold synopsis for an affidavit:

- Write a brief synopsis of the main point of the affidavit and identify the affiant.
- Keep the synopsis to 40 or 50 words.
- Put the synopsis up front, indented, and in boldface type.

A bold synopsis for the original affidavit might look like this:

This affidavit, by Kenneth Ivey's supervisor, Dennis Ragley, explains that Ivey was demoted because he missed his shift — after his cat died — and because he did not find someone to cover his shift. Ivey's demotion was not based on his being male.

This bold synopsis tells the reader, in a brief and forceful way, the critical point of the affidavit, right up front. Beginning affidavits this way benefits both the writer and the reader.

The writer benefits because creating the bold synopsis makes you think hard about what you're asserting in the affidavit. The bold synopsis helps you focus your writing on the critical point. It makes you articulate your point, succinctly.

Readers benefit because the bold synopsis allows them to quickly grasp the point of the affidavit even if they do not have time to read the whole thing. But for readers, the bold synopsis is more than just a time-saver. When readers scan the bold synopsis before reading the main text, it becomes easier to follow the story in the affidavit; the story makes sense the first time through. Plus, when the ending is spelled out up front, readers tend to fit the story to the ending — and that's persuasion.

I grant that the bold synopsis makes the affidavit look unconventional, and it might seem unusual to have an affiant provide a summary as part of the testimony in the affidavit. But neither of those concerns prevents you from including a bold synopsis. The bold synopsis will save enough judicial time that you'll be thanked for being unconventional.

2. Use headings to ease the reader's way.

To make affidavits more readable, easier to follow, and more inviting to the eye, use headings.

- Put headings in boldface type so they stand out.
- Use some topic headings (one or two words each).
- Use some phrasal headings—cogent phrases that preview the factual assertions.

Headings in affidavits can be very effective. They cue the reader about content and organization. They break up long blocks of text. They make documents easier to skim. Most lawyers know headings work well in motions, briefs, and contracts. Then why don't lawyers use headings in affidavits? Well, you may be thinking, affidavits are a written form of testimony. No one testifies using headings—it's odd.

But no one testifies with paragraph numbers, either, yet nearly all affidavits use them. Let's be clear: an affidavit is not a transcript of testimony—you don't put questions and answers in it. Instead, an affidavit is a statement of facts in writing sworn to by the affiant. It's a prepared document: written out, thought over, polished. So why can't you use headings in an affidavit?

You can. Here's the original affidavit with headings added:

The affiant

1. My name is Dennis Ragley. I am over 21 years of age, of sound mind, and I have personal knowledge of the facts stated herein. I am the District Supervisor for ReadyFoods, Inc., and I am responsible for 10 restaurants in the south Texas area, including the Beaumont Freddy's restaurant.

Events surrounding Ivey's demotion

2. On July 10, 1999, I was contacted by Celia Gonzales, an assistant manager at the Beaumont restaurant, and was informed that a shift manager, Kenneth Ivey, had called the restaurant and said that he would not work his scheduled shift because his cat had died that morning. In addition, Kenneth Ivey had not found someone to cover his shift during his absence.

3. I called Kim Henderson, who was originally scheduled to begin working at the restaurant as the General Manager on July 17, 1999, and asked if she would cover Kenneth Ivey's shift since he had not found anyone to cover his shift.

4. I also asked Kim Henderson to suspend Kenneth Ivey without pay until I could speak with the company's human resources department concerning proper discipline.

Reasons for Ivey's demotion

5. After speaking with Demetria Suka, the human resource administrator, and Ted Whitney, General Counsel for Ready-Foods, Inc., I decided that Kenneth Ivey should be demoted for failing to work his scheduled shift and for failing to find a person to cover his shift. The fact that Kenneth Ivey was a male had absolutely no bearing on my decision to demote Mr. Ivey.

6. No other employee has ever been given time off for the death of his or her pet.

7. Mr. Ivey was demoted because he had shown by his actions that he could not handle the responsibility of being a shift manager.

* * *

The addition of headings makes the affidavit easier to understand, easier to follow, and more persuasive.

3. Create a neat, clean look by eliminating formulaic clutter.

Too much of what gets passed on from old affidavits to new affidavits is archaic, formulaic clutter. For example, many affidavits begin with a caption like this:

STATE OF TEXAS   §

                          §

COUNTY OF TRAVIS   §

Does this type of caption have a name? (It's not a *jurat*.) Does anyone know why it's there? After all, the affidavit isn't going to be filed in the county's real-estate records. And, most important, is it required in an affidavit?

My informal survey of several dozen lawyers shows that they do not know what it's called, they're not sure why it's there, and they doubt it's required. After I surveyed those lawyers, I did my best to find out through researching on my own, and I found nothing. Until I know what it is and why it's there, it doesn't go in my affidavits. And I challenge you to follow me — if you don't know what it is, find out or don't put it in.

Another example, from the end of an affidavit, is the familiar phrase:

FURTHER AFFIANT SAYETH (or SAITH) NAUGHT (or NOT).

This archaic boilerplate actually does have an explanation. Fortunately, someone has done the research on this one, and he is a reputable source. Bryan Garner, in Garner's *Dictionary of Legal Usage*, tells us the phrase is from Elizabethan England — the late 1500s — and that English lawyers abandoned it long ago. I suggest that American lawyers today could well abandon this Elizabethan phrase too. So I agree with Garner's counsel on variations of the "further affiant" phrases: "The best choice, stylistically speaking, is to use these phrases not."[12]

---

12. Bryan A. Garner, *Garner's Dictionary of Legal Usage* 383 (3d ed., Oxford. U. Press 2011).

If we apply the techniques I've suggested here to the original affidavit, we greatly improve it:

- We get an up-front summary.
- We get easy-to-follow headings.
- We get a clutter-free, contemporary document.

Here's how the affidavit looks after applying the three techniques:

Affidavit

This affidavit, by Kenneth Ivey's supervisor, Dennis Ragley, explains that Ivey was demoted because he missed his shift—after his cat died—and because he did not find someone to cover his shift. Ivey's demotion was not based on his being male.

Dennis Ragley, under oath, says:

The affiant.

1. My name is Dennis Ragley. I am over 21 years of age, of sound mind, and I have personal knowledge of the facts stated here. I am the District Supervisor for ReadyFoods, Inc., and I am responsible for 10 restaurants in the south Texas area, including the Beaumont Freddy's restaurant.

Events surrounding Ivey's demotion.

2. On July 10, 1999, I was contacted by Celia Gonzales, an assistant manager at the Beaumont restaurant, and was informed that a shift manager, Kenneth Ivey, had called the restaurant and said that he would not work his scheduled shift because his cat had died that morning. In addition, Kenneth Ivey had not found someone to cover his shift during his absence.

3. I called Kim Henderson, who was originally scheduled to begin working at the restaurant as the General Manager on July 17, 1999, and asked if she would cover Kenneth Ivey's shift since he had not found anyone to cover his shift.

4. I also asked Kim Henderson to suspend Kenneth Ivey without pay until I could speak with the company's human resources department concerning proper discipline.

Reasons for Ivey's demotion.

5. After speaking with Demetria Suka, the human resource administrator, and Ted Whitney, General Counsel for Ready-Foods, Inc., I decided that Kenneth Ivey should be demoted for failing to work his scheduled shift and for failing to find a person to cover his shift. The fact that Kenneth Ivey was a male had absolutely no bearing on my decision to demote Mr. Ivey.

6. No other employee has ever been given time-off for the death of his or her pet.

7. Mr. Ivey was demoted because he had shown by his actions that he could not handle the responsibility of being a shift manager.

Signed:

* * *

In this revised affidavit, readers get a bold-synopsis summary right up front, highlighted headings to guide them through the story, and a clutter-free document that's easy to read and understand. This is an affidavit a judge can use.

Chapter 9

Writing to the Appellate Judge

- *State a well-framed issue up front.*
- *Use transitions and connectors.*
- *Avoid personal attacks.*

Hundreds of books and articles have been written on brief writing, and all of them try to help lawyers do a better job of writing to appellate judges and their staffs. Yet too many appellate briefs are still poor. Here's what judges say:

> A good one [a brief] is essential to appellate advocacy, but it is rare. — Hon. Roger J. Miner, United States Court of Appeals, Second Circuit.[1]

> Perhaps 50 percent of the briefs filed with our court are so one-sided and superficial as to be essentially discarded after an initial skimming. — Hon. Albert Tate, Jr., Supreme Court of Louisiana.[2]

> We simply don't have time to ferret out one bright idea buried in too long a sentence. — Hon. Ruth Bader Ginsburg, United States Supreme Court.[3]

This chapter offers three simple suggestions that will improve your appellate briefs.

---

1. Roger J. Miner, *Twenty-Five "Dos" for Appellate Brief Writers*, 3 Scribes J. Leg. Writing 21 (1992).
2. Albert Tate, Jr., *The Art of Brief Writing: What a Judge Wants to Read*, 4 Litigation 11, 11 (1978).
3. As quoted in Mark Rust, *Mistakes to Avoid on Appeal*, 74 ABA J. 78, 79 (Sept. 1988).

1. State a well-framed issue up front.

In *The Winning Brief*, the legal-writing expert Bryan Garner says "every brief should make its primary point within 90 seconds."[4] Judges agree. For example, Judge Nathan Hecht, of the Texas Supreme Court, has encouraged lawyers to lead with a statement of the issue:

> Start in the very first sentence with the problem in this case. Put it right up front. Start early. Don't bury it under a lot of verbiage and preliminaries.[5]

Judges say they often read the issue statements first—even if they're not up front—to get a sense of the case. So don't make the judge hunt to find the issues. If the judge wants to read the issues first, then make it easy; place the issue statements, prominently, at the beginning of the brief (within the limits of the court's required brief format, of course).

Besides placing issues up front, which many local briefing rules require, phrase them in a way that is tailored to the type of question they present. This helps the judge easily grasp the issue. In tailoring the question, I offer the following advice for two broad types of questions: (1) if the question is one of law (what the law is or what legal standard applies), phrase the issue statement briefly and generally, omitting facts; (2) if the question is one of application (how the law applies to a set of facts), phrase the issue in multiple sentences with factual specificity.

Some specific guidance:

First, the question of law. To write an effective issue statement for a question of law, I recommend the following approach. Use a short issue statement and frame the issue generally. Do not narrate the facts. If the question can be framed as a single sentence, do it. If it takes a couple of sentences, that's fine, too. Strive for concision—boil

---

4. Bryan A. Garner, *The Winning Brief* 48 (Oxford U. Press 1999).

5. As quoted in Bryan A. Garner, *Judges on Effective Writing: The Importance of Plain Language*, 73 Mich. B.J. 326, 326 (1994).

it down and make it understandable on a first reading. Here are two examples:

Question of law for a memo

> In assessing liability for a participant-on-participant sports injury, will the defendant's duty be measured under the reckless-intentional standard of care or the inherent-risk standard of care?

Question of law for a brief

> In assessing liability for a participant-on-participant sports injury, was the defendant's duty properly measured under the reckless-intentional standard of care?[6]

Second, the question of application. To write an effective issue statement for a question of how the law applies to a set of facts, I believe the best way is to use the "deep issue," an approach Garner advocates. He says a well-written issue statement should:

- Consist of separate sentences.
- Contain no more than 75 words.
- Incorporate enough detail to convey a sense of story.
- End with a question mark.[7]

Take special note of the first bullet. Garner abandons the traditional and, I say, old-fashioned approach to framing issue statements—the single-sentence format. That form is dying out, and I'm here to push it along. I've been teaching my students to write multiple-sentence issue statements since 1997. Other than tradition, there just isn't anything to commend the single-sentence issue statement for questions that require applying law to facts. The only way to make them worse is to begin them with "whether," like this one. I took it from a legal memo addressing an age-discrimination case.

---

6. Wayne Schiess & Elana Einhorn, *Issue Statements: Different Kinds for Different Documents*, 50 Washburn L.J. 341, 356 (2011).

7. Bryan A. Garner, *The Deep Issue: A New Approach to Framing Legal Questions*, 5 Scribes J. of Leg. Writing 1, 1 (1994–1995).

> Whether an employee who was told he was being fired for
> failing a physical, and who, after the 180-day deadline for fil-
> ing an age-discrimination claim with the EEOC had passed,
> heard talk that the firing was age-based and then one week
> later saw a memo that demonstrated a discriminatory mo-
> tive, can toll the time limits so that his filing after seeing the
> memo will be timely?

Honestly, it's not a grammatical sentence but a fragment that needs
three words at the beginning: "The question is ..." Plus, it's a single
sentence of 67 words — too long and too difficult to grasp on the first
reading. And the rule that the question must be stated in a single sentence has forced the writer to pile up several awkward clauses.

So join the contemporary trend toward the multiple-sentence issue
statement. Take a look at how effective that approach can be. I've
rewritten the age-discrimination issue statement here:

> Employees alleging age discrimination have 180 days to file
> a claim with the EEOC unless the delay is due to employer
> deception. John Erickson, 55, was told he was fired for fail-
> ing a physical, but after 180 days had passed he heard talk
> that his firing was age-based. A week later he saw a memo
> suggesting a discriminatory motive. Can Erickson toll the
> time limits so that his filing after seeing the memo will be
> timely?

This example uses a flexible formula I recommend for writing fac-
tually oriented issue statements in office memos, which are generally
not intended to be persuasive. A formula for creating this type of
issue statement is —

- Start with a sentence that summarizes the relevant rule of
  law — briefly.
- State the key facts in a condensed way.
- Pose a legal question that can be answered yes or no.

This formula works well for an objective memo.

For a persuasive document like an appellate brief, I recommend a
slightly different formula:

- Start with a sentence that casts your side in a favorable light.

- State the key facts favorably, fairly, and briefly.
- Pose a question that can be answered yes or no.

Here's another pair that shows a traditional and multiple-sentence approach using the formula for an appellate brief:

Traditional

> Does Alamo Rent-a-Car have a duty to warn tourists of the risks of high crime in parts of Miami where Dutch tourists Gerrit and Tosca Dieperink visited Miami and rented a car from Alamo, and where they then got lost in Miami and where, while stopped at a gas station to ask for directions, Tosca Dieperink was shot and killed in a robbery attempt?

Contemporary

> Gerrit and Tosca Dieperink, Dutch tourists, stopped at a Miami gas station for directions, and Tosca was shot and killed during a robbery attempt as she sat in their Alamo rental car. Gerrit sued Alamo for failing to warn him that there was a high crime risk in parts of Miami. Does Alamo have a duty to warn foreign tourists of high crime areas?

Notice that instead of the "law, facts, question" formula of the objective issue statement, the contemporary, multiple-sentence version omits a statement of the law and emphasizes facts that are favorable to Gerrit Dieperink.

As you can see, the traditional, single-sentence format used by most brief writers is more difficult to read, more difficult to write, and gets the brief off on stilted footing. If you're going to lead with your issue statement—and you should—write it clearly, directly, and in the contemporary style.

2. Use transitions and connectors.

Your brief, even if it addresses a tedious subject, can be pleasant to read if you lead the judge through it easily and smoothly with plenty of transitions and connectors. To see how this suggestion works, consider these two passages taken from a brief. The first is the original; the second is a revision. Citations to authority are omitted. Ask yourself which is easier to read and why:

Original

> The trial court erred in holding that Alamo had a duty to warn the Dieperinks about driving in Miami. In the absence of a special relationship, no duty exists to warn against the criminal acts of third parties. Car-rental firms are not considered common carriers in Florida. Their relationship with their customers is distinct from that of other common carriers and the "special relationships" recognized by case law.
>
> A duty to warn exists only when the threat is foreseeable and creates an unreasonable risk of harm. The threat to the Dieperinks was not foreseeable because Miami crime rates had recently dropped. The Tampa rental agency could not be expected to know the crime situation in Miami. The lack of foreseeability is further evidenced by the industry practice not to warn tourists about the dangers of driving.
>
> The threat of harm was not unreasonable. The Dieperinks' car was not marked as a rental. Criminals could not use the car to target the Dieperinks as tourists. Tourists do get lost, so by removing the rental designations from the car, Alamo had done the only effective thing it could do to protect its customers.

Revision

> The trial court erred in holding that Alamo had a duty to warn the Dieperinks about driving in Miami. **That duty**— to warn of the criminal acts of third parties—does not arise in the absence of a special relationship. **Here** the only special relationship that might have been present is the one recognized by case law for common carriers. **But** in Florida, car-rental firms are not considered common carriers.
>
> Without a special relationship, a duty to warn exists only when the threat is foreseeable and creates an unreasonable risk of harm. **Here** the threat to the Dieperinks was not foreseeable **for three reasons. First**, Miami crime rates had re-

cently dropped. **Second**, the Tampa rental agency could not be expected to know the crime situation in Miami. **Third**, industry practice was not to warn tourists about the dangers of driving.

Not only was the threat unforeseeable for those reasons, the risk of harm was not unreasonable because the Dieperinks' car was not marked as a rental. **Thus**, criminals could not use the car to target the Dieperinks as tourists. **Of course**, tourists do get lost, but by removing the rental designations from the car, Alamo had done the only effective thing it could do to protect its customers.

The revision uses several techniques, and it provides transitions and connectors at the sentence level as well as the paragraph level. Specifically:

- If a sentence uses an important word or phrase, repeat that word or phrase—especially at the beginning of the next sentence—to allow faster recognition that the new sentence builds on the previous: *duty, common carrier, foreseeable*.
- Use demonstrative pronouns, like *that*, to tie a word or phrase to the preceding idea: *that duty, those reasons*.
- Add single-word transitions that signal a contrast, tell the reader you're talking about our case, or show that you're elaborating on the previous point: *here, but, thus*.
- For ideas that have discrete parts, use overt set-ups: *The threat was not foreseeable for three reasons*. Then fulfill the expectation by using numbered or ordered sentences: *First, Second, Third*.
- Add transition sentences or phrases that connect to the previous idea and set up what is to come: *not only, of course*.

These methods may seem simple and obvious. But if so, why are so many briefs weak on transitions and connectors?

Perhaps it's the passage of time: it was way back in seventh grade that we learned how to write transition sentences (and topic sentences, too). Have we forgotten? Or perhaps it's payback: in law school you read a thousand judicial opinions; often they were hard to follow and required a lot of rereading—symptoms of poor transitions and missing connectors. So now that judges have to read what you write, you're giving what you got.

Maybe. But more likely you're writing under harsh deadlines and you don't have time to polish the brief and add the transitions and connectors. Working under a tight deadline is the rule in law practice, so you can't change that. What to do? Two things.

First, get an early start on at least one project and take the time to read and edit it once strictly for transitions and connectors. Pay close attention to flow; ask someone not familiar with the case to read it and point out the bumps and hiccups. Edit accordingly. This idea is really a way of getting some intense practice. You may have time to do it only once or twice, but the more times you go through an edit solely for transitions and connectors, the more they become second nature. Soon writing with strong transitions won't require the extra time—which you don't have.

Second, list the techniques you used and the words you added on your transition-and-connectors edit. Keep that list by your computer or near where you write. It's your "transitions and connectors checklist." Glance at it as you write; incorporate the ideas into your text. Soon, you'll internalize the use of transitions and connectors to create smoothness and flow in your briefs, and you'll spend less time editing for them.

3. Stay away from personal attacks.

If you're angry about your case and outraged at the injustice visited upon your client, you have several people to vent on. You can attack the judges—the trial judge who ruled against you or the appellate judge you're addressing—and you can attack the opposing side—the lawyer or the party. But don't.

Attacking judges is a bad idea.

If you're going to attack or criticize a judge, it's usually the trial judge. After all, the trial judge may have ruled against your client and caused this appeal. Now you're angry or frustrated. So why not write bluntly about the trial judge's weaknesses and blunders?

One good reason to use a civil tone is that judges know each other, says Margaret Johns in *Professional Writing for Lawyers*: "The judge reading your appellate brief may have just returned from a camping trip with the judge you are attacking. Your attack on a friend will turn the court against you."[8] And even if they're not friends, judges tend to be protective of their judicial comrades, even those on lower courts.[9]

And remember you're appealing the judgment, not the judge.[10] Attacking or criticizing the trial judge is an ineffective technique for showing the flaws in the ruling, the reasoning, or the judgment. Rather, you should "show respect for the lower court," says writing expert Steven Stark, "even while questioning its ruling."[11]

What do judges consider to be attacking or criticizing? Many appellate-brief writers might be surprised to learn that judges have a low threshold. For example, Stark offers this advice from U.S. Court of Appeals Judge John Minor Wisdom:

> Do not say "the district court failed to consider" or anything like it. Treat district judges tenderly.[12]

So follow Judge Wisdom's advice and take it easy. You won't score points by attacking judges.

Attacking opposing counsel is bad idea.

Nearly every book on appellate-brief writing mentions this advice. Here it is from Myron Moskovitz, an experienced appellate lawyer, in

---

8. Margaret Z. Johns, *Professional Writing for Lawyers* 234 (Carolina Academic Press 1998).

9. Dennis Owens, *Appellate Brief Writing in the Eighth Circuit*, 57 J. Mo. B. 75, 82 (March/April 2001).

10. *Id.*

11. Steven D. Stark, *Writing to Win: The Legal Writer* 161 (Main Street Books 1999).

12. *Id.*

his book *Winning an Appeal*: "Many judges place a high value on professional courtesy, and they can become quite annoyed with an attorney who appears to be wantonly patronizing or demeaning to opposing counsel."[13]

But maybe the best way to drive home the point is to tell you what judges say:

> Next on the list of deadly sins come[s] ... personal attacks. — Hon. Christine M. Durham, Utah Supreme Court.[14]

> Appellate judges are not helped in their work by criticism of the ethics of the other lawyers in the case. Your criticism diminishes you in the eyes of the judges. — Hon. Robert E. Seiler, Missouri Supreme Court.[15]

> [U]nless it is actually material to the issues on appeal, it is usually not a good idea to point out the shortcomings of opposing counsel, since to do so risks arousing skepticism in the judge as to the rest of the brief. — Hon. Alice M. Batchelder, U.S. Court of Appeals, 6th Circuit.[16]

> Examples of no-nos ... include general allegations that the author's opponent "misstated issues and arguments raised by appellants," "made selective and incomplete statements about the evidence," and "distorted the causation issue." Judges' eyes glaze over as we read that kind of prose. — Hon. Patricia Wald, U.S. Court of Appeals, D.C. Circuit.[17]

So don't risk causing that glaze. Be temperate. Let your well-framed issue statement — right up front — and your lucid, well-connected prose win the case; personal attacks won't.

---

13. Myron Moskovitz, *Winning an Appeal*, 39 (3d ed., Michie Butterworth 1995).

14. Christine M. Durham, *View from the Bench: Writing a Winning Appellate Brief*, 10 Utah B.J. 34, 36 (Oct. 1997).

15. Owens, *Appellate Brief Writing in the Eighth Circuit*, 57 J. Mo. B. at 82 (comments of justice Robert E. Seiler of the Missouri Supreme Court).

16. Alice M. Batchelder, *Some Brief Reflections of a Circuit Judge*, 54 Ohio St. L. J. 1453, 1458 (1993).

17. Patricia Wald, *19 Tips from 19 Years on the Appellate Bench*, 1 J. App. Prac. & Process 7, 21–22 (1999).

Chapter 10

Writing to the Consumer

- *Translate jargon.*
- *Target readability.*
- *Test the text.*

In your legal work, do you ever write for consumers? For example:

- If your client sells a product, have you ever written a safety warning?
- If your client has a website, have you ever written a website disclaimer?
- If your client owns a venue, have you ever written a limitation of liability for the tickets?

For those situations and more, the primary audience is consumers. Today, legal writing intended for consumers is everywhere, and lawyers write for consumers frequently. This chapter suggests three key ways to improve legal writing intended for consumers, or what I call *consumer drafting*.[1]

To support the suggestions here, we'll focus on this limitation of liability, taken from the back of a baseball ticket and typical of consumer drafting:

THE HOLDER IS ADMITTED ON CONDITION, AND BY USE OF THIS TICKET AGREES, THAT HE WILL NOT TRANSMIT OR AID IN TRANSMITTING ANY DESCRIPTION, ACCOUNT, PICTURE OR REPRODUCTION OF THE BASEBALL GAME OR EXHIBITION TO WHICH THIS TICKET ADMITS HIM. BREACH OF THE FORE-

---

1. Wayne Schiess, *The Art of Consumer Drafting*, 11 Scribes J. Legal Writing 1 (2007).

GOING WILL AUTOMATICALLY TERMINATE THIS LI-
CENSE. THE HOLDER ASSUMES ALL RISK AND DAN-
GERS INCIDENTAL TO THE GAME OF BASEBALL IN-
CLUDING SPECIFICALLY (BUT NOT EXCLUSIVELY)
THE DANGER OF BEING INJURED BY THROWN OR
BATTED BALLS AND AGREES THAT THE PARTICIPAT-
ING CLUBS, THEIR AGENTS AND PLAYERS ARE NOT
LIABLE FOR INJURIES RESULTING FROM SUCH
CAUSES. THE MANAGEMENT RESERVES THE RIGHT
TO REVOKE THE LICENSE GRANTED BY THIS TICKET.

I'll call this text the *limitation*, and at the end of this chapter I'll present a complete and thorough revision. Now, the three suggestions.

1. Translate jargon.

Most consumers are not lawyers, so legal jargon—defined as language that lawyers use to communicate with each other[2]—should not
be used in consumer drafting. *License* and *agent* are two examples of
legal jargon in the limitation that are acceptable when writing for
lawyers but that might be confusing to consumers:

license	To a lawyer, it means permission to enter property when it would oth-erwise be trespassing. For example, entering a sports arena—which is private property—without a ticket would be trespassing, but the ticket holder has a license. Lawyers understand that. But the nonlegal defin-ition is a permit to own or use something. You need a license for a dog, a gun, or a car. That's likely to be the kind of "license" a consumer thinks of.
agent	To a lawyer, it's someone authorized to act for someone else. It's a broad term, and lawyers know there's a large body of law developed on agency. But as used in the limitation, it can be misunderstood. The lawyer who wrote the limitation surely meant to limit the liability of all those who act for the management. But consumers could justifiably

---

2. Bryan A. Garner, *Garner's Dictionary of Legal Usage* 490 (3d ed., Oxford U. Press 2011).

assume that agent means sports agent—it is, after all, a baseball game—and that would be a narrower limitation of liability.

Eliminate jargon words or translate them into everyday English. To identify these dual-meaning words, consult David Mellinkoff's *Language of the Law*, in which he lists 29 of them,[3] including

action	the process of doing; but to a lawyer, a lawsuit
consideration	careful thought; but to a lawyer, something of legal value
service	the act of helping; but to a lawyer, delivery of a summons

Carefully examine your draft for words that have one meaning to lawyers and a different meaning to consumers—legal jargon. Cut the jargon.

2. Target readability.

To improve the readability of the text in our limitation, you can rework the limitation from three perspectives.

Typographic readability

First, get rid of the ALL-CAPITALS typeface. If you want to draw attention to text, but still have it be inviting and readable, use bold-face for emphasis instead of all-caps. When every letter is uppercase, the text becomes harder to read, according to Robin Williams in her *Non-Designer's Design Book*.[4] Plus, all-capitals typefaces are often interpreted as shouting in print. Don't shout at the consumers who use your product or attend your event.

---

3. David Mellinkoff, *The Language of the Law* 11–12 (Little, Brown & Co. 1963).

4. Robin Williams, *The Non-Designer's Design Book: Design and Typographic Principles for the Visual Novice* 18, 109 (Peachpit Press 1994).

Second, carefully balance your type size and the number of characters per line. Generally, type sizes of 6 or 7 points are probably too small for consumer documents, but you may need to use 8- or 9-point type sometimes because of space limitations. If you must use small type, the number of characters per line of text becomes important. Try not to exceed 70 characters (letters and spaces) per line. Break the text into columns if you must, but avoid excessive characters per line because, as Garner notes, "the reader's eye tends to get lost … in moving from the end of one line to the beginning of the next."[5]

Third, know the difference between serifed and sans-serif typefaces, and choose the type you want. Serifed typefaces have—no surprise—serifs: shorts strokes extending from the ends of the main strokes. Here are three serifed typefaces:

Constantia

Garamond

Times New Roman

Sans-serif typefaces have no serifs, like these:

Arial

Calibri

Verdana

For shorter texts, sans-serif typefaces are fine. They will give the text a contemporary and informal feel, thus making the text more inviting. But for longer texts, serifed typefaces will be easier to read[6] and will come across as more formal and professional.

And avoid Courier, a nonproportional typeface that will make your documents look like they were created on a typewriter.

Word and sentence readability

The guru of readability was Rudolf Flesch. Lawyers who must write for consumers should keep his book, *How to Write Plain Eng-*

---

5. Garner, *Garner's Dictionary of Legal Usage* at 291–92.
6. *Id.*

lish: A Book for Lawyers and Consumers, on their desks. In it, Flesch explains his readability formula, an index that rates a text for readability based on word length in syllables and on sentence length.[7] On the Flesch scale, zero is "very difficult," and 100 is "very easy." Under his formula, a text must score 60 to be considered "plain English" or what I call good consumer drafting. (MS Word can calculate the Flesch readability score for you.)

The readability score for our original limitation is 35 — only a few points better than a typical law-review article and well below the threshold for good consumer drafting. Because the score is based on word and sentence length, let's first identify some long words to replace, and then address the sentences. Try to eliminate or change these long words:

automatically

condition

exclusively

exhibition

foregoing

incidental

specifically

terminate

(I'm not providing suggested substitutes here, although *event* is a good substitute for *exhibition.* As you'll see, my proposed revision of the limitation eliminated most of these words instead of replacing them.)

Next, consider the sentences. The limitation has 109 words and four sentences, for an average of 27 words per sentence. That's not bad, but the longest sentence (the third one) is 47 words. Remember that in each sentence, you ask readers to hold the information in their heads until they reach the period. So the longer the sentence, the more you ask the readers to hold, and the more difficult it becomes.

---

7. Rudolf Flesch, *How to Write Plain English: A Book for Lawyers and Consumers* 20–26 (Harper & Row 1979).

Difficult reading is not what we're after. Lawyers drafting for consumers shouldn't ask too much of consumers. Instead, deliver the meaning as easily as possible, in readable, manageable sentences. It's easy to improve the sentence length in our limitation; just break the longest sentence into two:

> The holder assumes all risk and dangers incidental to the game of baseball including specifically (but not exclusively) the danger of being injured by thrown or batted balls.

> The holder agrees that the participating clubs, their agents and players are not liable for injuries resulting from such causes.

That simple revision alone improves the readability because the average sentence length drops to a respectable 22 words. And merely by dividing one sentence into two and shortening the average sentence length, you raise the readability score to 40.

Using "you" for readability

To write well for the consumer audience, you must use the word *you*. The expert, Flesch, called it "The Indispensable You," and devoted a whole chapter to it.[8] The more you resist the second-person *you*, the more stilted and stuffy your writing will become. You end up using phrases like *the holder*, or you use the masculine pronouns *he* and *him* when you obviously mean to include women.

In the limitation, the use of *you* improves readability greatly; it focuses the reader's attention because it makes the text apply to the reader in a concrete way:

Instead of	Write
the holder assumes	you assume
the holder agrees	you agree

---

8. Flesch, *How to Write Plain English* at 44–50.

I think using *you* in consumer drafting is the single most important technique for making the text readable and effective. It has the effect of making the document speak to the reader, giving the content immediacy and concreteness. To use it effectively, you'll need to define you early in the document, but that's fine. In my drafting courses, I always notice a marked improved in student work once they get past the fear of using *you*.

3. Test the text on the audience.

To draft effectively for consumers, you must get a draft of your document done early enough to run it by some nonlawyers. You need input from the intended audience. Steven Stark, author of *Writing to Win: The Legal Writer*, says your writing should pass the *McDonald's test*: "If you were to read the document you're drafting aloud in McDonald's, would people understand what you're saying?"[9]

That's a good standard for consumer drafting. Ideally, you'd have a dozen typical consumers read the draft and give you responses. Ask your readers questions like these:

- Could you understand everything in the text?
- What was hard to understand?
- What words sounded like legal jargon?
- How easy was it to read?
- What does it mean?

When you ask your test audience those questions, you're likely to receive some criticism. That may hurt your ego a bit, but if you're determined to have the text understood, you need to welcome honest input from the intended audience.

In fact, I tested both the original limitation and a proposed revision on 20 nonlawyers. By the way, ten of them were confused about the meaning of *agent*, although only two were confused about *license*. Overall, 19 preferred the revision to the original.

---

9. Steven D. Stark, *Writing to Win: The Legal Writer* 36 (Three Rivers Press 2012).

A possible revision

Based on the responses from real consumers, and relying on the suggestions offered in this chapter, here's a possible revision of the limitation:

> This ticket admits you to the event listed on the front. By using it, you agree not to broadcast or help broadcast any descriptions or pictures of the event. If you do, you must leave the event.
>
> By using this ticket, you accept the risks of attending a baseball game. For example, you could be hit by thrown or batted balls or injured in other ways. Stadium management, its representatives, the teams, and the players are not responsible for your injuries.
>
> Management may revoke this ticket and remove you from the event.

The revision has 92 words, 13 words per sentence, and scores 65 on the Flesch readability scale—just right for consumer drafting. Of course, this draft isn't perfect, and it might not satisfy all lawyers, but it's a good example of how lawyers can improve the way they write for consumers.

Chapter 11

Drafting for the Transactional Lawyer

- *Drop the worst archaisms.*
- *Avoid known ambiguities.*
- *Impose obligations consistently, actively, and directly.*

When I was first asked to prepare a contract for a client, I immediately thought back to my Contracts class—in which I hadn't learned to draft a contract. That's probably true of nearly all lawyers: Contracts was about the law of contracts, not the drafting of contracts. So what did I do? I asked around for a form (also called a "template" and a "precedent"). Using forms in a transactional practice is standard. Indeed, if lawyers drafted all contracts from scratch, commerce might grind to a halt and clients would howl at the fees.

But forms have their drawbacks. Before I present the three tips in this chapter, I'll first highlight some things to keep in mind as you use forms.

Master the form. Read it, understand it, and know it. Proofread it thoroughly and be sure it contains what you need. Don't assume it perfectly fits the current transaction. For example, I once received a draft contract for the sale of a uranium-processing facility that referred to the sale of "the Restaurant." Oops.

Learn the deal. Even as a novice transactional lawyer, strive to understand the provisions in any form you use. In *Legal Writing in Plain English*, Bryan Garner points out the tremendous risk of sending opposing counsel a draft containing a provision you don't fully understand: You might be asked about it.[1] Don't take that chance. Study it, research it, and ask your supervisor.

---

1. Bryan A. Garner, *Legal Writing in Plain English* 117–18 (U. Chicago Press 2001).

Now, three tips for drafting.

[handwritten annotation: "Get rid of bad 'legalese.'"]

1. Drop the worst archaisms.

By the way, another drawback of forms is that they often perpetuate the worst of ancient legalese, and I do mean ancient. Some of the phrases still showing up in contracts today are from Elizabethan English—the 1500s. None that I'll mention here have any useful legal meaning, and some seem not to have any meaning at all. They're pointless.

Still, although they're pointless, they're also usually harmless. Most don't cause litigation or create ambiguities. So although I recommend cutting them all from your own forms, it may not be worth it to insist on cutting them from a draft contract sent over by opposing counsel. You could end up looking excessively pedantic.

And please don't believe the assertions of some lawyers who insist that clients expect archaic terms and legalese. They'd have you suppose clients want to be confused and baffled or that clients believe in magic words. As Susan Chesler, a legal-writing professor and drafting expert, suggests, transactional drafters should "think like an attorney, but try not to sound like one."[2] There's no data to support the assertion that clients prefer legalese, but there is empirical research showing that nonlawyers dislike it.[3]

Here's my list of archaic words and phrases that will never appear in a draft I prepare, and I hope you'll join me:

---

2. Susan Chesler, *Drafting Effective Contracts,* 19 Bus. Law. Today 35 (Dec. 2009).

3. Christopher R. Trudeau, *The Public Speaks: An Empirical Study of Legal Communication,* 14 Scribes J. Leg. Writing 121 (2011–2012).

Archaism	Commentary
aforementioned	Archaic but also vague; specify what you're referring to.
foregoing	Same comment: archaic and vague.
in witness whereof	Has no meaning in modern legal English.
know all men by these presents	Archaic, meaningless, and has the added drawback of being sexist.
now therefore (in recitals)	Unnecessary
whereas (in recitals)	Harmless but archaic. Label the recitals as such (or as *Background*) and narrate the information in normal prose without the archaisms.
wherefore premises considered	Still shows up in court documents but also appears in contracts. Pointless.
witnesseth	"To make WITNESSETH shout in all capitals from the top of a document makes no literal sense."*

* Bryan A. Garner, *Garner's Dictionary of Legal Usage* 950 (3d ed., Oxford U. Press 2011).

In making these recommendations, I've focused on only the worst archaisms and haven't suggested removing other stuffy legalisms: vague *here-* and *there-* words like *herein, therein,* and so on; outdated pronouns and demonstrative pronouns like *said, same,* and *such*; and other phrases like *duly, henceforth, that certain, wheresover,* and *to wit.* But I've abandoned them, too.

Whatever you do, take a stand for modern legal language and banish these unnecessary, archaic words and phrases from anything you draft.

2. Avoid known ambiguities.

Ambiguity is undesirable in legal drafting, and a good legal drafter will identify and eliminate as much ambiguity as possible. Ambiguity—a single expression susceptible of two incompatible meanings—is different from vagueness—a lack of specificity. Vagueness is inevitable and sometimes necessary in legal drafting: *good faith* efforts, *material* change, *reasonable* time. It's worth distinguishing the concepts.

Designating time periods sometimes results in ambiguity. In general, avoid designating time periods with *by* and *until*, like this:

Seller shall deliver the products by April 1, 2013.

Licensee is authorized to use the Licensed Rights until May 31, 2013.

In these provisions, it's unclear whether the specified date is included in the time period. In other words, if the Seller must deliver *by* April 1, does that allow delivery *on* April 1? The same with *until*: is the specified date included? A better approach is to use *on or before*.

Seller shall deliver the products on or before April 1, 2013.

For even more precision, Kenneth Adams, the author of *A Manual of Style for Contract Drafting*, recommends specifying a time and location.[4]

Licensee's authorization to use the Licensed Rights ends at 5:00 p.m., Austin, Texas time, May 31, 2013.

Two other types of recurring ambiguity arise when a modifying word or phrase is placed before or after a textual list. The first type is sometimes called a *leading modifier* or *pre-modification*, and looks like this:

The Trustee may fund charitable hospitals, schools, and foundations.

The ambiguity arises because it's possible for *charitable* to modify all three items in the list (hospitals, schools, foundations) or for *chari-*

---

4. Kenneth A. Adams, *A Manual of Style for Contract Drafting* 186–88 (2d ed. ABA 2008).

table to modify only the first item, the one that immediately follows it (hospitals).

Careful drafters spot these leading modifiers and revise to clarify. Depending on the intended meaning, you can move the modifier, repeat the modifier, or place the modifier to lead into a tabulated, numbered list.

Move the modifier

> The Trustee may fund hospitals, schools, and charitable foundations.

Repeat the modifier

> The Trustee may fund charitable hospitals, charitable schools, and charitable foundations.

Tabulate and number

> The Trustee may fund charitable
>
> (a) hospitals,
> (b) schools, and
> (c) foundations.

A related type of recurring ambiguity arises when a modifying word or phrase appears after a textual list. This type is sometimes called a *trailing modifier* or *post-modification*, and looks like this:

> To qualify for advancement, the candidate must be within the weight range for his/her height, score eighty-five (85) on the first test battery, score ninety (90) on the special-placement battery, and achieve an eighty-five percent (85%) accuracy score on the shooting range within six weeks of application for advancement.

Here the ambiguity arises because the trailing modifier, *within six weeks of application for advancement*, could modify all four preceding requirements or only the fourth requirement (85% on the shooting range).

Again, careful drafters spot trailing modifiers and revise to eliminate ambiguity. Depending on the intended meaning, you can move the modifier and add clarifying language, create separate provisions, or place the modifier to lead into a tabulated, numbered list. (And while we're at it, let's delete the repeated text and numerals and use only the numerals.)

Move the modifier and add clarifying language

> To qualify for advancement, the candidate must, within six weeks of application for advancement, complete all the following: be within the weight range for his/her height, score 85 on the first test battery, score 90 on the special-placement battery, and achieve an 85% accuracy score on the shooting range.

Create separate provisions

> (1) To qualify for advancement, the candidate must be within the weight range for his/her height, score 85 on the first test battery, and score 90 on the special-placement battery.

> (2) To qualify for advancement, the candidate must, within six weeks of application for advancement, achieve an 85% accuracy score on the shooting range.

Tabulate and number

> To qualify for advancement, the candidate must, within six weeks of application for advancement,

> (a) be within the weight range for his/her height,
> (b) score 85 on the first test battery,
> (c) score 90 on the special-placement battery, and
> (d) achieve an 85% accuracy score on the shooting range.

3. Impose obligations consistently, actively, and directly.

A key part of any contract is the language that imposes the contractual duties. For example, in a simple contract for the sale of goods, the fundamental obligations would be for the buyer to pay the price and for the seller to deliver the goods. A well drafted contract will impose those obligations consistently, actively, and directly.

Be consistent in phrasing obligations. I believe all the obligations in a contract should be imposed using the same language—but it's not my idea. It's a near-universal truth of drafting: when you intend the same idea, you should use the same language. In *Drafting Legal Documents*, Barbara Child put it well, advocating

> the crucial drafting technique of saying the same thing the same way throughout a document to prevent a reader from thinking that slightly different phrasings are purposefully intended to refer to different things.[5]

Drafters should strive for consistency, particularly when relying on forms received from others. Often, a single form document has been assembled from several other forms, all prepared by different drafters at different times. Too often, confusing inconsistencies creep in. For example, in an oil-and-gas lease I once received, the drafter used (or allowed) three different phrases for creating contractual obligations:

Lessee *will* pay royalties ...

Royalties *shall be* paid monthly ...

Lessee *agrees to* provide reports ...

Why phrase these obligations differently? Although the different phrasings aren't likely to cause significant problems, they do invite a question: Is there a difference between saying someone *will* do something and saying someone *agrees to* do something? And what about saying something *shall be* done? All three should be phrased using the same binding word or phrase. In my view, part of a drafter's job when using a form is to regularize the language.

Use the active voice when phrasing obligations. When you use the passive voice to impose contractual obligations, you either multiply words unnecessarily or, worse, you fail to make clear who has the obligation. Consider these two examples:

1. On the closing date, the purchase price shall be paid.
2. On the closing date, the purchase price shall be paid by the Buyer.

---

5. Barbara Child, *Drafting Legal Documents* 75 (2d ed. West 1992).

The problem with number 1 should be obvious: the obligation to pay the purchase price is not actually imposed on anyone. That's a result of one of the effects of the passive voice: the subject of the sentence is no longer performing the action of the verb. So in number 1, no one is obligated to pay—it just happens. Don't draft this way.

Number 2 at least puts the obligated party back into the sentence, but it does so by adding that party to a prepositional phrase at the end. As a result, the sentence is longer than it needs to be and lacks the force of the active voice. Don't draft this way.

Yes, the passive voice has its uses in analytical and persuasive writing—and might even be appropriate in some drafting contexts—but it's not appropriate for imposing contractual obligations. Use the active voice: "The Buyer shall pay . . ." That's better.

Impose obligations directly. You might think that as long as you use the active voice to impose obligations, you'll be fine, but there's one more thing to keep in mind. Here's the problem I encountered in a divorce decree (yes, divorce decrees are a form of legal drafting):

Petitioner shall receive 25% of the net proceeds of Respondent's bonus checks.

As you can see, the obligation here is for the Petitioner to *receive* the proceeds, when it should be for the Respondent to *pay* them. Surely a judge construing the language would enforce the obligation to pay the bonus-check proceeds to the Petitioner, but the language here does not literally impose that obligation. Don't draft this way.

I recommend imposing all obligations in a drafted document with consistent terminology, in the active voice, and directly on the party to be obliged. To draft obligations consistently, actively, and directly, I suggest this approach:

(1) Use either *shall* or *agrees to* (other words can work, like *promises to* and *will*, but *shall* and *agrees to* are good choices and are common).
(2) Phrase the obligation in the active voice.
(3) Impose the obligation on the party to be obligated.

Here are three examples:

(1) Lessee shall [agrees to] pay Royalties on all Proceeds of the oil or gas produced from the Leased Premises.

(2) On the closing date, the Buyer shall [agrees to] pay the purchase price.

(3) Respondent shall [agrees to] pay Petitioner 25% of the net proceeds of Respondent's bonus checks.

Ultimately, you're responsible for the drafted documents you prepare, even if you relied on an old form. Take the time to make the form your own by understanding it and adapting it appropriately to the current transaction.

Chapter 12

Writing for the Citizen

- *Format for easy reading.*
- *Shun legalisms and formality.*
- *Use short sentences.*

In your practice, do you ever need to write for the typical citizens—the real people who need to read and understand the rules that apply to them? That kind of writing is usually legislative and regulatory drafting, a narrow specialty within legal drafting. Most lawyers probably assume they never need to write for the citizen. But ask yourself:

- Have you ever written or revised the bylaws for an organization? (When I volunteered to serve in my neighborhood association, that's the first thing they asked me to do.)
- Have you ever needed to draft public rules? (I was once asked to revise the rules for using the local cable-access channel.)
- Have you ever needed to draft a declaration that the parties understand their rights and obligations?

In all of those situations you're writing for the audience of "citizens." So you need to understand that audience and adapt to its abilities, expectations, and needs. For example, most citizens are not lawyers, and some will have limited education. How will you write effectively for them? This chapter presents three simple suggestions to improve legal writing intended for citizens.

First, read this legislatively enacted "statement on alternative dispute resolution," taken from the Texas Family Code:

I AM AWARE THAT IT IS THE POLICY OF THE STATE OF TEXAS TO PROMOTE THE AMICABLE AND NON-JUDICIAL SETTLEMENT OF DISPUTES INVOLVING

CHILDREN AND FAMILIES. I AM AWARE OF ALTERNA-
TIVE DISPUTE RESOLUTION METHODS, INCLUDING
MEDIATION. WHILE I RECOGNIZE THAT ALTERNA-
TIVE DISPUTE RESOLUTION IS AN ALTERNATIVE TO
AND NOT A SUBSTITUTE FOR A TRIAL AND THAT
THIS CASE MAY BE TRIED IF IT IS NOT SETTLED, I
REPRESENT TO THE COURT THAT I WILL ATTEMPT IN
GOOD FAITH TO RESOLVE BEFORE FINAL TRIAL CON-
TESTED ISSUES IN THIS CASE BY ALTERNATIVE DIS-
PUTE RESOLUTION WITHOUT THE NECESSITY OF
COURT INTERVENTION.[1]

This statement was once required in the first pleading filed by each
party in suits affecting the parent-child relationship and in divorce
suits. The statement had to be "prominently displayed in boldfaced
type or capital letters or be underlined and be signed by the party."[2]

I'll call that text the *statement*, and I'll offer my three suggestions
in the context of that statement. Afterward I'll present a complete revision of the statement. Now, the three suggestions.

1. Format for easy reading.

When writing for the citizen audience, remember that the format
of the text is critical. The visual presentation can make the text either
inviting or intimidating. Keep in mind these formatting suggestions:

Use a readable typeface.

The first thing to change is obvious, and I've said it before: change
the ALL-CAPS to boldface type. That is, after all, the first option
listed in the statute. If you want to draw extra attention to the language, you can put a box around it.

---

1. Tex. Fam. Code Ann. § 102.0085(a) (Vernon Supp. 2002) (repealed).
2. Tex. Fam. Code Ann. § 102.0085(b), § 6.404(b) (Vernon Supp. 2002).

Break up long blocks of text.

The original statement is a solid block of unbroken text. Even after converting it to regular type, it can be off-putting:

> I am aware that it is the policy of the State of Texas to promote the amicable and nonjudicial settlement of disputes involving children and families. I am aware of alternative dispute resolution methods, including mediation. While I recognize that alternative dispute resolution is an alternative to and not a substitute for a trial and that this case may be tried if it is not settled, I represent to the court that I will attempt in good faith to resolve before final trial contested issues in this case by alternative dispute resolution without the necessity of court intervention.

So lawyers writing for citizens should use numbering and white space to break up this block of text and make it more accessible. After all, this statement is important — the citizen readers need to be able to understand it, so help them by formatting it in digestible chunks. Try this:

1. I am aware of

    (a) the policy of the State of Texas to promote the amicable and nonjudicial settlement of disputes involving children and families, and

    (b) alternative dispute resolution methods, including mediation.

2. While I recognize that alternative dispute resolution is an alternative to and not a substitute for a trial and that this case may be tried if it is not settled, I represent to the court that I will attempt in good faith to resolve before final trial contested issues in this case by alternative dispute resolution without the necessity of court intervention.

We may need further textual revisions to make this new format work well, but even as it is, the text is more inviting, simpler to read, and easier to understand.

2. Avoid legalisms and formality.

Legalisms and formalisms are the old, stuffy, fancy words and phrases that characterize legal writing. Not only do they distract and confuse the citizen reader, they often cause unwarranted intimidation. This statement should bring about comprehension, not intimidation. So when you're writing for the citizen audience, mercilessly weed out legalisms and formalisms.

The original statement is full of legalisms and formalisms. For example:

Replace these words and phrases	With these words and phrases
I am aware	I know
amicable	peaceful
non-judicial settlement	out-of-court settlement
alternative dispute resolution	non-court solution
represent	promise
contested issue	dispute (or case)
court intervention	court action

If you carefully scrutinize your drafts for legalistic and unnecessarily formal words, you'll produce a clearer and more understandable text.

3. Use short sentences.

The original statement is 98 words long and has three sentences—for an average sentence length of 33 words. Consumer-drafting expert Rudolf Flesch says lawyers ought to strive for an average sentence length of 20 words.[3] At 33 words per sentence, this statement has room for improvement.

---

3. Rudolf Flesch, *How to Write Plain English: A Book for Lawyers and Consumers* 24 (Harper & Row 1979).

Plus, the longest sentence in the statement—the third one—is 62 words. That's too long for the citizen audience. Even though an occasional sentence of 40 or 50 words can be manageable, once a sentence goes over 50 words, it becomes difficult to follow.

And please remember that "difficult to follow" is a relative term. We lawyers are used to long sentences; we began reading them in our casebooks in law school. But for the typical citizen, the statement's average sentence length, and the third sentence in particular, are more difficult than necessary.

To improve sentence length and readability, simply break the third sentence into two, like this:

> I recognize that alternative dispute resolution is an alternative to and not a substitute for a trial and that this case may be tried if it is not settled.

> I represent to the court that I will attempt in good faith to resolve before final trial contested issues in this case by alternative dispute resolution without the necessity of court intervention.

That simple revision improves readability by decreasing the average sentence length to 25 words. But we can do more. Next, consider a full revision of the statement.

The revision.

Based on the suggestions in this chapter, and after testing some drafts on typical citizens, I wrote this revision of the statement:

By signing this statement, I affirm that:

1.   I know that Texas promotes peaceful, out-of-court settlements of family-law cases.

2.   I know about non-court solutions, including mediation.

3.   I know that non-court solutions are an option and not a substitute for a trial.

4.   I know that this case may go to court if it is not settled.

5.   I promise to try—in good faith—to resolve this case out of court.

In this revision, there are 71 words, with an average sentence length of 12 words. The readability is greatly improved. But some lawyers will doubtless have concerns. Let me address two.

First, I eliminated the phrase *alternative dispute resolution*. Most lawyers know what it means, but most typical citizens do not. (Try asking a nonlawyer.) To work around that phrase, I used variations of the phrase *settle out of court*.

Second, to some lawyers, the phrase *settle out of court* is redundant because all settling is "out of court." But in my survey of 50 typical, nonlawyer citizens, more than half thought *settle* meant **any** resolution — even when the judge resolved the dispute. Only *settle out of court* clearly conveyed the meaning that the settlement was without the judge's involvement. Thus, *settle out of court* conveyed the desired meaning more clearly.

Perhaps some lawyers and legislators will not want to go this far in revising the statement. That's not surprising; most lawyers will have different comfort levels with the tone and format of legal writing that is intended for citizens. But what's surprising is how often we lawyers forget our audience. This revision is just one example of how lawyers can improve the way they write for citizens.

Chapter 13

Writing for the Screen Reader

- *Summarize.*
- *Enable skimming.*
- *Be brief.*

Today, many judges, lawyers, supervisors, and clients will read your writing on a screen instead of on paper. In fact, many courts now require lawyers to submit all filings electronically. In *Legal Writing for the Rewired Brain*, Robert DuBose asserts that readers behave differently reading on the screen when compared to reading on paper.[1] I think he's right, and if you want to succeed as a lawyer writing for screen readers, you should learn the traits of screen readers and write accordingly.

According to the research DuBose consulted, we can make the following generalizations about screen readers:

- Screen readers get impatient,[2] and tend to spend less time on a screen document than they would on a printed document.
- Screen readers skim a lot,[3] even more than when reading a printed document.
- Screen readers show a top-left preference: they focus more on text at the screen's top and left and less on text at the bottom and right. The preference is called the F-pattern[4] because the screen reader's eyes move in a pattern that resembles an uppercase F.

---

1. Robert Dubose, *Legal Writing for the Rewired Brain: Persuading Readers in a Paperless World* (2010).
2. *Id.* at 42.
3. *Id.* at 39.
4. *Id.* at 37.

Given these tendencies, what can legal writers do when writing for screen readers? The advice is not surprising and, frankly, would benefit print readers, too.

1. Summarize.

At the top of the document, as early as the rules and conventions allow, summarize your main points or give the answer with reasons or state your request and support it — whatever the document calls for. In short, provide a substantive summary. I recommend a substantive summary rather than a mere roadmap ("Part A presents.... Part B discusses....") because the impatient screen reader wants the goods, not just a description of where to find the goods. A substantive summary that doubles as a roadmap is even better. Do it by presenting the substantive points in the order they'll appear in the document's body.

Here's an example from a motion for summary judgment:

Summary

Naca, Inc. is entitled to summary judgment on all former employee Susan Freeman's claims. Freeman's state and federal sexual-harassment claims fail because she cannot show she was subjected to severe or pervasive harassment. Her retaliation claim fails because Naca has produced evidence of legitimate, non-discriminatory reasons for disciplining and terminating her. Freeman's vicarious liability claims against Naca for the alleged assaults of another employee fail because the employee was not acting in the course and scope of his employment when he allegedly assaulted Freeman — and Naca never ratified his actions. Finally, Freeman's negligence claims are barred because Naca is a workers' compensation subscriber.

Notice that the summary is labeled with a boldface heading so the reader can quickly spot it. It's thorough — mentioning four causes of action and giving a reason each one fails. Yet it's succinct — it's been boiled down, with details saved for later. Finally, it presents these causes of action in the same order in which they'll be addressed in the Argument section of the motion.

You can also include a mini-summary for every major section of the document and even a single-sentence summary for every paragraph—a topic sentence.

2. Enable skimming.

I recommend accommodating the heavy skimming screen readers do by making your documents easy to skim. The primary way to make a document easy to skim is with headings. Headings facilitate skimming, allowing the screen reader to skip ahead easily and quickly.

When adding headings, legal writers use these two types: (1) Main headings (also called section headings or topic headings), which are usually a single word or a short phrase that describes the subject or topic of that portion of the text, like *Summary, Statement of Facts, Argument,* and *Conclusion.* (2) Explanatory headings (also called assertive headings or point headings), which are usually complete sentences that summarize a topic, explain an idea, or assert an argument or claim.

By rule or convention, many legal documents already require main headings and explanatory headings. For example, in an appellate brief, the main headings divide the brief into separate sections, and assertive point headings assert claims or propositions that will be supported in the text. Naturally, these enable skimming. But other legal documents can benefit from the skim-ability of headings, particularly explanatory headings: e-mail, letters, articles, newsletters, and more.

In using headings, here are three things to keep in mind.

First, aim for brevity, not bulk. Remember that if the headings are to enable skimming, the reader must be able to grasp their essence quickly. Cut extraneous details and streamline the headings so they're succinct. Avoid bulk. Be brief. Consider these before-and-after examples:

Bulky

a. Freeman's sexual-harassment claims, which she brought under Title VII of the federal Civil Rights Act and the Texas Commission on Human Rights Act ("TCHRA") must both fail on the basis that she has not and cannot produce evidence that, while employed at Naca, she was subjected to severe or pervasive harassment based on her sex.

Better

a. Freeman's harassment claims under Title VII and the TCHRA fail because there is no evidence she was subjected to severe or pervasive harassment based on her sex.

Second, left-align your headings. Given the top-left preference and the skimming tendency, aligning headings and subheadings on the left margin helps screen readers. Headings on the left margin are easy to skim — they line up along the left margin, the place a screen reader's eye naturally falls. Centered headings are harder to skim. Although centering your main headings is harmless, even they can be placed on the left margin. Never center explanatory headings like the point-headings in a brief or motion.

Third, make your explanatory headings stand out. To aid the screen reader in differentiating levels, apply a consistent numbering system, use contrasting typefaces (boldface, italics, or bold italics), or indent each lower heading level one additional tab length. In addition, be sure to create alignment in the headings:

(1) Don't have the subsequent lines of text go all the way back to the left margin, like this.

(2) Use the indentation function — different from a mere tab — so subsequent lines of text align with first line, like this.

(3) Don't over-indent; if you indent three or more tab lengths, you'll destroy the left alignment that eases skimming.

AND DON'T USE ALL-CAPITALS TEXT. Any readability and skim-ability advantage you gain from left alignment is lost if the headings are in all-capitals text.

3. Be brief.

Accommodate screen readers' brief attention spans with a brief document. But let me clarify: what I advocate here is better called concision. To be brief simply means to write less, to make it shorter, and anything can be made shorter by cutting content. To be concise means to make your writing as short as possible while preserving content. Sure, some content deserves cutting. But don't cut crucial content. Instead, preserve necessary content while using as few words as possible. Be concise.

Ultimately, think about how you read on the screen. Write and lay out your text in a way you'd like to read.

Chapter 14

A Word about Citation

I've tried something different with the citations in this book, and I hope you won't even notice. But just in case you're curious, I explain myself here.

1. I've used the *ALWD Citation Manual.*

The citations in this book were prepared according to the *ALWD Citation Manual.*[1] The *ALWD Manual* was published in 2000 by a group of legal-writing professionals, the Association of Legal Writing Directors (ALWD, pronounced "all wood") and Darby Dickerson, an expert in legal citation. They designed it to compete with *The Bluebook.*[2] To read about the creation of the *ALWD Citation Manual*, visit ALWD's website: <www.alwd.org>.

The *ALWD Manual* does not present a new system of legal citation. Instead, it presents a system nearly identical to *The Bluebook* system, but it does so in a reader-friendly, clearly written, and well-designed text. That's the advantage of the *ALWD Manual*: the rules are easy to read and follow, the text is well organized, and it offers supplemental guidance on citation that *The Bluebook* does not.

Citation form under the *ALWD Manual* does differ — slightly — from *Bluebook* form in some minor ways. The major difference is that the *ALWD Manual* uses the same form for law review style and prac-

---

1. Association of Legal Writing Directors & Darby Dickerson, *ALWD Citation Manual: A Professional System of Citation* (4th ed. Aspen L. & Bus. 2010).
2. *The Bluebook: A Uniform System of Citation* (Columbia L. Rev. Assn., *et al.* eds., 19th ed. 2010).

titioner documents. If you're silent for a moment, you'll hear a swelling cheer going up from lawyers across the country—especially from legal-writing teachers like me. Under the *ALWD Manual*, citations will be in the same style whether they appear in a law review or a book or a trial brief or an office memorandum.

The Bluebook requires different styles or "typeface conventions" for citations depending on whether they appear in law-review footnotes or in practitioner documents. This distinction has caused problems for law students and lawyers for decades. Few lawyers ever completely master the separate systems, and the two systems make *The Bluebook* itself unnecessarily complicated.

The main difference between the two *Bluebook* typeface conventions is the use of LARGE AND SMALL CAPITALS in law-review footnotes, but not in practitioner documents. The *ALWD Manual* has wisely banished LARGE AND SMALL CAPITALS from its citation system. One system of legal citation no matter the type of document: it's great.

As a practical matter, the existence of different typeface conventions in *The Bluebook* was a relic of the time when practitioners used typewriters but law reviews were professionally printed. Typewriters can't produce LARGE AND SMALL CAPITALS (or *italics* for that matter). Thus, the two systems developed. In this book, for example, a citation to a book will look like this:

Gary Blake & Robert W. Bly, *The Elements of Technical Writing* 141 (Macmillan 1993).

and not like this:

GARY BLAKE & ROBERT W. BLY, THE ELEMENTS OF TECHNICAL WRITING 141 (1993).

I don't see the need for the LARGE AND SMALL CAPITALS typeface. We all have access to the same typefaces as professional printers. And the *ALWD Manual*'s authors wisely decided to abandon the differences altogether.

2. I've written so you won't need to check the footnotes.

My goal in preparing this book was to make the text flow and still include plenty of authority for the tips I've offered. But often, including a lot of authority means the text won't flow; instead, the reader can get bogged down by in-text citations. That's typical of legal writing—we lawyers often insert long, hard-to-read legal citations into our text, unintentionally creating "hiccups" for our readers.

To avoid that, I put the citations into footnotes. The references are there, so you have access to the authority. Putting citations into footnotes is also typical for books, not to mention scholarly articles.

But many readers like to know what authority supports an idea or assertion, and they want to know it now, without having to consult the footnotes. To accommodate those readers, I've consistently included a short reference to the authority in the body text and placed the bibliographic details in a footnote. That way, readers get the source information now and can look up the detailed citation later.

For example, here the reader meets a long and distracting citation (a big hiccup) after the quotation:

It is still possible to be too informal, particularly with email:

Since E-mail is so informal, there is a tendency to write in short, staccato sentences and phrases; to keep the message in all capital letters; and generally to ignore the rules of punctuation and spacing. Appearance still counts. Treat your E-mail the same as any other professional communication.

Gary Blake & Robert W. Bly, *The Elements of Technical Writing* 141 (Macmillan 1993).

On the other hand, in the next example, the reader learns nothing about the source of the quotation and must check the footnotes if curious about the source:

It is still possible to be too informal, particularly with email:

Since E-mail is so informal, there is a tendency to write in short, staccato sentences and phrases; to keep the message in all capital letters; and generally to ignore the rules of punctuation and spacing. Appearance still counts. Treat your E-mail the same as any other professional communication.[3]

But in the final example, the reader gets the authors' names and a shortened title of the book from which the quotation was taken—in the body text. Yet the detailed bibliographic information is saved for the footnote:

It is still possible to be too informal, particularly with email, as pointed out by Gary Blake and Robert W. Bly in their book, *The Elements of Technical Writing:*

> Since E-mail is so informal, there is a tendency to write in short, staccato sentences and phrases; to keep the message in all capital letters; and generally to ignore the rules of punctuation and spacing. Appearance still counts. Treat your E-mail the same as any other professional communication.[4]

This is the approach I've chosen. My goal is to provide identifiable authority throughout the text yet still make the text as readable and smooth as possible.

---

3. Gary Blake & Robert W. Bly, *The Elements of Technical Writing* 141 (Macmillan 1993).

4. *Id.*

Index

summary, 16, 33, 34, 61, 63,
66-68, 70, 74-76, 82, 88, 89,
126, 127
table of authorities, 65
table of contents, 65
tabs, 128
tabulation, 78, 79
test, 107
therein, 111
tone, 31, 32, 37, 44, 48-56, 58,
59, 63, 65, 99, 124
transactional lawyer, 109-117
transition, 44, 97
transitions, 95, 97, 98
trial, 47, 48, 59, 73-89

trial brief, 63, 64, 75, 76
trial judge, 73-89
type size, 70, 104
typeface, 70, 103, 120, 132
typefaces, 70, 103, 104, 128,
132
uppercase, 103
usage, 8, 9, 38, 44, 87, 102
usage dictionary, 8
vogue word, 9
website disclaimer, 101
whereas, 111
white space, 69, 70, 121
witnesseth, 111
you, 106-107